The English Civil War

Three and a quarter centuries ago Englishmen fought Englishmen to determine whether their nation was to be ruled by king or parliament. As with most civil wars, victory did not automatically establish the original principles of the victors. The Royalists, led by cavaliers with long hair set in ringlets, were defeated by the Parliamentarians, whom they derided as "Roundheads," because they wore their hair cut short. Yet, it was many years after the execution of King Charles in 1649 before true parliamentary government evolved in England.

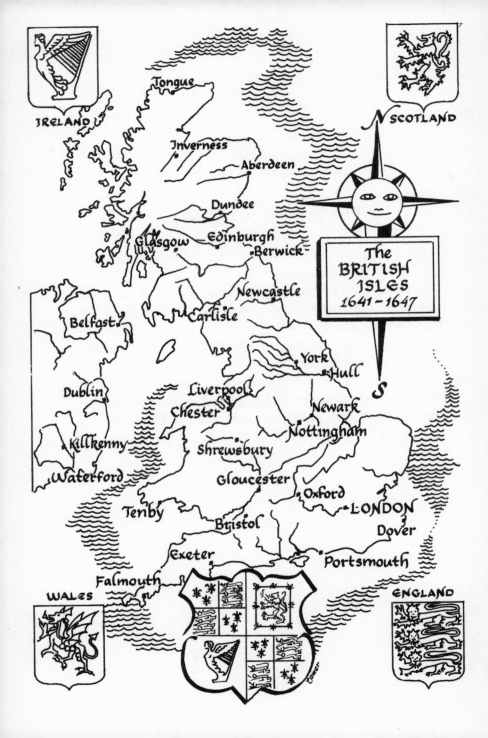

The English CIVIL WAR

**By
Sutherland
Ross**

**G. P. Putnam's Sons
New York**

Contents

Contents

Foreword

Any writer producing a book on the English Civil
War must be indebted to the many scholars and
authors who have done so much work on the
subject. To them my grateful thanks are due.

Special acknowledgment is owing to the Bodleian
Library, Oxford, for permission to quote from the letters
of M.S., and to the Kent County Council for material
quoted from the excellent book, *Kent and the Civil War,*
produced by the County Archivist and his staff.

The picture of the medallion of Charles I has been re-
produced by kind permission of the Trustees of the
British Museum, and the portraits of Pym, Cromwell
and Fairfax are from the National Portrait Gallery,
which has kindly allowed their use.

The English
CIVIL
WAR

I

Battle Royal

"Lord, Thou knowest how busy I must be this day. If I forget Thee, do not Thou forget me. . . . March on, boys!"

So prayed old Sir Jacob Astley on the morning of October 23, 1642. It was a Sunday, a suitable day for prayer, but not for the other work Sir Jacob had in hand.

His last three words had been spoken to the nine thousand foot soldiers whom King Charles had been hastily collecting during the previous weeks. Now, on

KING CHARLES I

this bright cold morning, they were stumbling down the green steepness of Edgehill to take up positions on the gentler slopes below.

Elsewhere in England the bells were calling people to church. Here, in Warwickshire, the lively drums were beating on the air.

A long-threatened day had dawned at last. On the wide plain below, between King Charles and his highway to London, stretched a dense hedge of men, glinting with steel and flecked with banners.

Down the hill, smearing the muddy grass, went the

King's Foot. A man who watched them that day wrote down later what he saw.

"Most had muskets and powder bags and pikes. No pikeman had armor and few musketeers had swords."

They had no uniforms either, but were still wearing the smocks or doublets they had been wearing at home a few weeks before. They could, however, drill a bit and shoot after a fashion. Come what might, they meant to stand their ground.

The King's Horse were better supplied. From the manor houses of England and Wales they had come riding at their king's call. They had taken from their family armories the swords, pikes and muskets that their grandfathers had handled against the threat of Spain's Armada some fifty years before.

With these they had armed their retainers and marched away. They had been bred from infancy to use their own swords and manage their mounts in rough country. If there was more to warfare than that, they were content to learn it as they went along.

Down the hill they went on this October day. Three abreast, with harness ajingle, their horses delicately paced the slope. Then, wheeling in troops, they passed like shadowed clouds across the hillside.

To the Earl of Essex, who was waiting in the valley below, those clouds of horsemen spelled a day of storm and fury. He was facing a battle he had not expected in a cause which must have begun to puzzle him.

The enemy he now saw coming down the hill was fighting for the king, and they knew exactly what it

EARL OF ESSEX

meant. But the Earl of Essex was fighting for the king
... *and Parliament*. Neither he nor anybody else in
England quite knew what that meant.

It could hardly mean, for instance, firing a cannon
upon the King's Own Majesty. Yet this, it seemed, was
what the poor earl must do.

The burst of cheering from the rapidly forming enemy line, the brave scarlet of the lifeguards and the pale
droop of the Royal Standard all told him that King
Charles was facing him in person.

Perhaps that was why the Earl of Essex waited for so
long before beginning the battle. Perhaps he was waiting for the rest of his army, strung out along the road

a day's march behind. But wait he did, while the autumn day warmed slightly under the climbing sun.

The delay gave a certain hawk-nosed young man the chance to ride from one side of the king's army to the other. At every troop of horse he paused awhile and spoke earnestly to the riders.

They leaned eagerly forward in their saddles to catch his words. He was only twenty-three, and a foreigner at that. But he was nephew to the King of England and had already spent ten years of his short life in warfare. Prince Rupert of the Rhine, handsome, experienced and bold, was well worth listening to. One of his hearers wrote down what he said:

> [The Prince] passed from one wing to the other giving positive orders to the Horse to march as close as possible, keeping their ranks with sword in hand; to receive the enemy's shot without firing either carbine or pistol till we broke in amongst the enemy and then to make use of our firearms as need should require; which order was punctually obeyed.

Both armies were now ready, the king's infantry ranged in lines six-deep and his eager cavalry on the wings. The Earl of Essex had placed his cannons along the Parliamentary front, protected by more than a thousand dragoons and musketeers.

In the flash and rumble of his guns the battle began.

The Royalists, with fewer guns, made swift reply. But as the clouds of black smoke drifted between the armies they saw that Essex had the advantage. His shot was tearing holes in their ranks, but their own cannons were firing too high. In vain they tried to depress the reeking muzzles; the slope of the ground defeated them.

The king's dragoons were now ordered forward. They began to engage the Parliament men who were protecting those punishing guns. The enemy gave ground slowly.

All this, however, had been only the overture to the battle. Now one of the main instruments was brought into play. The right wing of the King's Horse, commanded by Prince Rupert, was on the move.

The trumpets blared; the light shone on sword and breastplate, on curling plume and scarlet sash. Knee to knee, the Cavaliers rode down the slope and onto the level ground, turning inward as they went so as to strike the enemy from his left front.

The opposing horsemen rode out to meet them, one troop well in the lead and firing its pistols wildly in the air. Then, to its comrades' dismay, its men stripped themselves of Parliament's orange sashes and turned to ride with Rupert. That troop, commanded by Sir Faithful Fortescue, had changed sides.

In the next moment Prince Rupert struck. His horsemen burst upon the enemy with slashing swords and a deadly hail of pistol shot. The Parliament Horse broke into a frightened rabble that fled toward its own hapless infantry.

A man called Holles, a famous Member of Parliament, saw his four hundred musketeers ridden down by

16

PRINCE RUPERT

their panic-stricken friends. Next to them, more foot soldiers broke into confusion and fled without being charged.

The whole left wing of the Parliamentary army had been ruined. With wild yells and loosened reins, Prince Rupert's men galloped in pursuit.

On the other side of the battlefield the day was not going much better for the king's enemies. The royal cavalry there was commanded by Lord Wilmot. He had advanced more slowly over difficult ground which was intersected by a hedge lined with musketeers.

17

In spite of their fire he gained the hedge and rode onward to attack the right wing of the enemy's cavalry. Before long they too were in flight and Wilmot was chasing them off the field. Even the king's own reserve, which was supposed to protect his person, was carried away by excitement and now joined the jubilant pursuit.

It must have seemed to both Wilmot and Rupert that the battle was already won. But most of the foot on both sides had stood firm. Sir Jacob Astley, judging the time to be ripe, ordered the king's line to advance.

An eyewitness tells us what happened then.

> When the royal army was advanced within musket shot of the enemy, the foot (infantry) on both sides began to fire, the king's still coming on and the rebels only continuing to keep their ground; so that they came so near to one another that some of the battalions were at push of pike . . . insomuch that the Lord Willoughby with his pike killed an officer of the Earl of Essex's own regiment.

The battle was now like some fatal game of chess in which the larger pieces had been swept from the board. The foot were doggedly fighting it out on equal terms, heaving and stabbing at each other with their fearsome pikes and using their clubbed muskets at close quarters.

Although the King's Horse had been victorious he had lost the use of it. Indeed, his position was now worse than that of the Earl of Essex.

One of the attackers wrote later: "So we got up to the

greatest part of the enemy's ordnance, cutting off the gears of the horses that drew them, and killing the gunners under the carriages."

King Charles was facing disaster. His left flank was gone and he and his two sons were in danger. Just ahead of him he could see his standard, ringed around by the enemy, but bravely held aloft by old, white-haired Sir Edmund Verney.

Then Verney fell. With a yell of triumph the enemy seized the standard. All seemed lost except courage. The King's Foot retreated but did not break.

The Prince of Wales, a boy aged twelve, and his brother James, aged nine, were now only a few yards from the attacking horsemen.

A man called Hinton, who was in charge of them, implored the two princes to leave the field. But the blood royal of England and Scotland was running warmly in Prince Charles's veins.

"I fear them not!" he shouted defiantly, and drew his pistol with a view to charging the foe.

An enemy trooper caught sight of him and spurred his horse forward to seize so rich a prize. Shots were exchanged and the attacker fell from his horse. The future Charles II was saved.

Meanwhile a man with the homely name of John Smith was earning himself a knighthood. He charged the men who were bearing away the standard and in fierce fight managed to wrest it from them.

Two of the royal regiments now exerted themselves to save the day.

"They retired orderly and at last made a stand; and having the assistance of cannon and a ditch before them, held us in play very handsomely." So said one of their enemies, paying generous tribute to courage. But the courage was high on both sides, for these were men of one nation and of a common blood. When all else was gone, this remained.

Another eyewitness tells us: "Each, as by mutual consent, retired some paces and then stuck down their colors, continuing to fire at one another even until night."

As the sun went down the firing gradually died away, but neither army would budge from the field. In the chilly twilight, the king's errant cavalry returned with jaded horses and weary men, too late to be of any use.

Their wild chase after the enemy had brought them little profit. They had burst into the village of Kineton, expecting to find a rich and easy plunder of Parliamentary wagons, but they had met with a warm welcome.

The baggage train was being guarded by troops under the command of John Hampden, a man who had already proved his courage in the struggle against the king. His men stood firm. Their fire took a stiff toll of the enemy, and the roughly handled Cavaliers went in search of easier prey.

By evening, the first battle of the Great Rebellion had been fought but not won. The only prizes to be picked up from the field of Edgehill lay in the lessons it held for those who had the wit to learn.

It had shown that the men of Britain, fighting on foot,

are not easily dismayed. A thousand years of history, of battles like Hastings and Crécy and Agincourt, had already shown the same.

But Edgehill had proved more than that. It had shown that victory would go to the side which first learned to handle its cavalry properly.

One man had learned a third lesson. He spoke to his cousin, John Hampden, soon after the battle. His words were full of contempt for the Parliamentary horsemen that had fled the field.

"Your troopers," he said, "are most of them old decayed servingmen and tapsters and such kind of fellows. You must get men of spirit that are likely to go on as far as gentlemen will go or else I am sure you will be beaten still."

The man who spoke was already looking for such men of spirit and was forming them into a troop. He was Captain Oliver Cromwell.

OLIVER CROMWELL

II

A London Apprentice

With the darkness came bitter cold. Amid the ranks of the two weary armies men sought their friends. Others moved slowly among the fallen, finding here and there some wounded man to comfort.

The cruel frost itself saved one. Sir Jervase Scroope, lying with seventeen wounds on him, was found still alive. Only the cold had stopped him from bleeding to death.

But neither night nor harsh weather forced either army from the field. Throughout the darkness the soldiers stamped the ground with numbed feet and beat their hands together for fleeting comfort.

There was time that night for thinking and regretting. Many must have wondered what had brought them and their country to this.

One of these was, perhaps, a merchant's apprentice called Nehemiah Wharton. We have his letters, written to his master back in London, and we know that he was in the Parliamentary army shortly before the battle.

In one of his letters he had complained about his colonel. He wrote: "We all desire that either Parliament should depose him or God convert him or the Devil fetch him away quick."

The colonel, it appears, was not a very religious man, and Nehemiah was. He knew exactly what he was fighting against. In another letter, he says: "We came to Wendover, where we refreshed ourselves and burnt the rails."

Nehemiah meant the communion rails, which the clergy under orders from Archbishop Laud had been erecting in the parish churches. When Nehemiah and his comrades entered a town, this would be their first task: to invade the church, throw out the altar, burn the communion rails and perhaps indulge in a little shooting practice at any images they might find carved upon the stonework.

Today, in some of England's churches, angels with

chipped wings and effigies with scarred and battered faces are there to remind us of what such men as Nehemiah were willing to do.

Sometimes, however, there were accidents. This one, reports Nehemiah, happened at Wendover, too: " . . . Accidentally, one of Captain Francis's men, forgetting he was loaded, shot a maid through the head and killed her."

To us, nowadays, these seem strange deeds for religious men to do. But Nehemiah, like his fellows, was quite certain that he was fighting the battles of the Lord. He had spent his youth as an apprentice to George Willingham, a London merchant who lived at the sign of the Golden Anchor in St. Swithin's Lane. In that house there was a great deal of Bible reading and family prayers. There would be visits, as well, to church, where the congregation would sit enjoying sermons that sometimes lasted for three hours. It was no wonder that Nehemiah knew the Ten Commandments by heart.

One of them, especially, was in his mind when he marched through England with the Earl of Essex.

Thou shalt not make unto thyself any graven image. . . .

That was what the Bible said. That commandment was the Word of God.

Yet King Charles and his Archbishop Laud had been allowing such things. Indeed, the Archbishop had gone even further. He had tried to force honest folk to turn toward the altars when they prayed.

For Christians, thought Nehemiah, the Lord's Table

24

should be enough. Those altars were heathen things, decked out with candles and such Popish nonsense. There was a proper place for that Table, out in the church and not hidden away and guarded with rails at the eastern end of the building. The white-robed priests, too, looked more like heathen Druids than decent Christian ministers. As for prayers, they ought to come from a man's heart, not out of a book written by bishops.

These thoughts were in Nehemiah's mind when he saw what Archbishop Laud was doing. He and his comrades were quite certain that they knew what Laud was planning. He was out to bring Popery back into England, and it was all to please the king's Roman Catholic wife.

Nehemiah was determined that it should not happen. It was less than a hundred years since the papist Queen Mary had been burning men and women at Smithfield. Nehemiah had read all about it in Foxe's *Book of Martyrs.*

What he had not read he could learn easily enough from the gossips who clustered around the conduits of the city when they went to draw water for their households. Or, on business for his master, he could pause awhile on one of the busy quays down by the river and listen to sailors' tales about the Spanish Inquisition.

The Thames was crowded with ships from all countries. Hundreds of ferryboats plied up and down from Westminster to the City or across the bright water to Bankside, where the theaters were.

Lads like Nehemiah found the river a pleasant

change from the narrow stinking little alleys in which many of them lived. The brisk smell of salt water, the warm reek of tar and the bearded sailors with their news from foreign parts all made it an exciting place to be.

If all other amusements failed, there was always London Bridge, carrying a whole street of houses and shops on its bank and standing, with its burden, knee-deep in the stream. The current, as the tide ran out, would pile up the water into high waves around its supports. It curved to rush through the arches in perilous waterfalls of glassy green. To see a boat shoot those rapids was a holiday in itself.

But there were other holidays as well, when Nehemiah and his friends could go to see the lions at the Tower of London or wander out into the fields and woods that still lay close to the city's walls.

There was always something to do, hard work or vigorous play; for London lay at the very hub of things and traded with the world.

The year 1642 had brought more holidays than usual for the lads and lasses of the city. Things were astir in Parliament. The pot that had been bubbling for fifteen years was about to boil over.

It started early in the year, on January 4th, when King Charles lost his patience and did something that no other English monarch had ever dared to do.

For many years he had ruled the country without calling a Parliament at all. He had levied unjust taxes and had flung into prison the men who would not pay. One of them, Sir John Eliot, had died pitifully in resisting him.

But Charles had been foolish enough to start a war against his people in Scotland. He had tried to force the rule of bishops upon them. The people of Scotland had banded themselves together and had sworn a Solemn Oath and Covenant to fight against him.

They had beaten him, too, and this had encouraged some of the English to copy their example. With his pockets empty, King Charles had been forced to call the English Parliament. Its members met together in angry determination.

They brought low the king's great minister, Thomas Wentworth, Earl of Strafford. They hated him for two reasons: first because he had once been their friend and had turned his coat; second, because he had helped the king in his tyranny by being so clever and thorough in his work.

With all Parliament against him, the Earl of Strafford had only the king to rely on. But the leaders in Parliament, especially John Pym, had brought out the London mob to threaten Queen Henrietta Maria. King Charles had given way and signed the earl's death warrant.

That was in 1641; but in January 1642, Parliament had tried to follow up its victory. The king then decided to arrest the ringleaders.

He forced his way into the House of Commons with armed men at his back and demanded the delivery of five of them. Their names were Pym, Hampden, Holles, Hazlerigg and Strode. Every one of them was a hero to Nehemiah Wharton and his friends. All of them, except Pym, were later to fight at Edgehill.

But on that January afternoon their danger was greater than in battle. Being warned in time, they fled from the Commons and took refuge in the city. The baffled king stared around at his angry Parliament and failed to find them.

"The birds are flown!" he cried before he stalked out.

Next day he began to search the city for them. The citizens and apprentices turned out in full force to defend their champions. Somebody who saw it happen wrote these words to a friend in the country:

The king had the worst day in London yesterday. People crying "Privilege of Parliament!" by thousands . . . shutting up their shops and standing at their doors with swords and halberds.

It must have been a grand day for Nehemiah Wharton, and there were more like it to come. A week later, knowing that London was ready to use armed force, King Charles left his capital. Everybody feared that he would never return without war. The rebel leaders began to make ready for it.

It was John Pym who was foremost in all their preparations. If anybody in England knew what was coming, it was John Pym. He was a man with a large, plump face and small intelligent eyes which seemed to miss nothing.

He had been a merchant and he knew how to make men do his will. Now he nerved them all to open revolt. Parliament began to raise armies by its own authority, a thing which was quite unlawful. Arsenals were seized and the lives of loyal citizens were soon made unbearable by gangs of men who roamed about and shouted for "King Pym."

In March, a peaceful petition from the gentry of Kent was presented to Parliament. The men who brought it were at once cast into prison. Others who spoke for King Charles were treated in a similar way.

In July 1642, before the war had started, a messenger from Parliament came riding from London to Bedford. One of the king's friends, Sir Lewis Dyve, was to be arrested. A neighbor of Dyve's, a man called Sir Samuel Luke, offered to assist in the arrest.

Sir Samuel was a very small man, but he seems to have been a plucky fighter. He rode off to Bromham Hall, where Sir Lewis Dyve was living.

Dyve refused to be arrested and began to fight. In the struggle Sir Samuel Luke received seven wounds, while Sir Lewis fought his way free, and escaped by swimming across the River Ouse. Both he and Luke lived to fight again.

Such things were happening nearly everywhere. In the north country, Sir John Hinton had his house plundered by a rabble. They seized goods to the tune of a thousand pounds and Sir John was forced to flee for his life.

But the king's side was also preparing for war. Before the attempt on Sir Lewis Dyve was made, Sir Lewis had ridden into Bedford and had boasted that he had five hundred bullets already cast for use against the Roundheads.

All over England both parties were seizing arms and horses from men who might tomorrow be enemies.

The trained bands of London were called out and began to drill in Bunhill Fields. They were citizens and apprentices who acted as part-time soldiers in normal times. When they met together there was often more beer and skittles than proper drilling.

But they were now in earnest and they were commanded by an old soldier, Philip Skippon. Their wives and daughters turned out to watch them. No doubt Nehemiah Wharton watched also as the armored pikemen marched ponderously up and down with their long, clumsy weapons. It is not surprising that Nehemiah decided he must join them.

This he probably did on July 26, when the excitement in London was intense.

A friend of the king's wrote later:

How forward and active the Londoners were to promote this rebellion can hardly be imagined; people of all sorts pouring out their treasure as if it had been for the most advantageous purchase in the world; throwing in with their plates and rings and not sparing their very thimbles and bodkins.

But all this was probably only the frenzy of a minority. There were still many people who felt nothing but horror at what was coming.

Seventy-seven Nottinghamshire gentlemen signed a petition for peace. Those midlanders spoke sense when they said: "We have ever been taught that all those laws made in Parliament consist of three estates, the commons, lords and king, and we think it dangerous to untwist that triple cord."

They were unhappily too late. The cord was already untwisted. Half the House of Commons had now been driven out of Westminster and only the rebels remained. King Charles was in the north, seeking almost in vain for arms and men.

To John Pym and his friends it must have seemed that the war was won before it had even begun. We can picture them in that rainy summer of 1642: a small band of determined men in sober doublets, sitting at tables in their paneled council chambers. They had gone too far to turn back. They had to break the king's power once and for all. Peace with Charles would put their necks in danger.

They had seized the arsenals of England. They had driven their enemies from London by unleashing the mob. What was worrying them now was the prospect of interference from abroad.

Queen Henrietta Maria was in Europe, badgering her kinsman the King of France for men and supplies. A dark-eyed, energetic and often stupid woman, she was hated in England for being a Papist. Surely, she thought, she could get help from the Roman Catholics abroad.

But, to Pym's joy, the sailors of the navy, who hated France almost as much as they hated Spain, now declared for Parliament.

It meant that any meddlesome foreigner would now have to face the guns of England's fleet in England's narrow seas. The kings of France and Spain answered Henrietta Maria with smiles and empty words. They remembered the Armada.

Henrietta turned from them in scorn. She had jewels to pawn and a desperate, willful courage in her heart.

Somehow she managed to get supplies through the blockade.

It was little enough, at that. Enough to break her husband's spirit if his spirit could be broken at all. For Charles had raised unlawful taxes to pay for the very fleet that had now gone over to the enemy.

The navy for which he had risked so much was using the winds of the ocean to wither his cause.

It was on the side of John Hampden, the man who had refused to pay Ship Money and was now using his great wealth to raise rebel troops in Buckinghamshire. Those troops were the ones who later gave Rupert such an unpleasant surprise at Edgehill.

Now they were drilling, while Nehemiah Wharton away in London was learning his new trade of soldiering on the worn and flattened grass of Bunhill Fields.

His lessons, however, must have been short. On August 9th King Charles made a proclamation, calling all men who could bear arms to rally by August 22nd at Nottingham. Only men who lived north of the River Trent were expected to come, but he collected few even of those.

Charles had only about six hundred men with him when August 22nd arrived. It was a wet and windy evening when he raised his Royal Standard. A strong gust of wind almost immediately blew it down again.

It was an evil omen, but it made no difference to the king's determination. Within the hour, the beacon fires of England were flaring the news from hilltop to hilltop. The sky was reddened with the sunset of peace.

Nehemiah Wharton must have seen those beacons. He may have been doing guard duty as the night came on. He was on his way to Coventry with the Parliamentary army.

Perhaps he was writing one of his letters by candlelight in the warm parlor of some friendly household. In one of the last messages he sent, he thanked his master for a scarf and hatband which had come "most seasonably." He went on to write that he had had a soldier's suit made for winter. It was "edged with gold and silver lace."

As he marched toward Edgehill along the miry roads of autumn, the young soldier must have looked brave and warlike in that new suit.

It is sad to think he may have died in it.

III

The Royalists

There were plenty of dead on both sides after Edge-hill, for it had been a big battle fought between two sizable armies. Yet, only a few weeks before, the king's forces had been no more than six hundred men. We cannot help wondering where all the others had come from.

Many had been waiting until it was certain that war had begun. Many more had changed their minds at the last moment when Parliament rashly threatened to abolish the Prayer Book.

The Book of Common Prayer was a part of nearly everybody's childhood. Men had been baptized by it and married by it. They were ready, if need be, to die for it.

"Dear Mother," wrote one youngster who had run away from his home in Cheshire. "It did much trouble me to depart from you as I did. . . . A true Protestant Christian was I born, baptized into the true faith of Christ, promised and vowed to maintain it, and by God's grace I will, to my last blood."

We do not know that young man's name because he signed only his initials — M.S. But M.S. survived Edgehill and lived to write other letters. We shall learn more about him later.

At his side in the battle were others who had thought hard before they rode to join the king. Their loyalty had overcome their scruples. One of these was old whitehaired Sir Edmund Verney.

He had no love for bishops and said so openly. But he could not desert the king in his hour of need. He joined King Charles, and died holding the standard at Edgehill.

Hundreds of the rest must have come without even thinking about it. They were country squires in whom the habit of centuries was strong. The king called, and his fighting men answered. It was as simple as that.

But roads were long, and there was grain to harvest before they set out, so they were slow in coming. When they did arrive they found that the bold and adventurous were there already.

Young men like William Holles, for instance. He was

twenty-one years old and eager to fight. He began first by pestering his uncle to enlist him. Then he rode to Nottingham on his own and sought out Captain John Smith.

Smith was an honorable man who had seen fighting abroad. He had no courtier's tricks and spoke little. But he knew a man when he saw one, so he took young William into his own company of foot.

William must have been there when John Smith saved the Royal Standard. But it is doubtful if he saw his captain knighted for the feat, for by that time William was blind.

In the battle he had been wounded severely in the face. His comrades urged him to leave the field, but he refused. He fought on until the end. Then he stumbled away with his face so swollen that he could not see.

He was like that for days afterward. Then he managed to force open one eye and was ready to fight again.

At Edgehill he had a kinsman fighting on the other side. His name was Denzil Holles and he was one of the five members of Parliament whom Charles had tried to arrest.

Denzil Holles had done little in the battle. His musketeers had been ridden down by their own frightened cavalry. In the cold darkness after the fight Denzil must have been feeling anxious.

Like John Hampden, he was quite sure that he was fighting for England's liberties. But he had memories that Hampden did not share. In the long years that were gone, Denzil had been King Charles's boyhood playmate. Perhaps he was remembering the shy, stammering young prince who had once been his friend.

If so, he was like many others that night who had parted in anger from friend or brother. They stared unhappily into the darkness and waited for the dawn.

Would the battle be renewed when the sun rose? John Hampden hoped so, and urged the Earl of Essex to attack. But Essex was feeling less bold. He wanted more to avoid a defeat than to gain a victory.

So Essex gave the order to retreat. With joyful eyes the Royalists watched the enemy depart. He left behind him a great deal of baggage and an open road to London.

The king that day dined upon a drumhead in the open. His cloaked and beribboned commanders gathered around him in council. Hands on sword hilts, they argued about what was to be done.

Rupert, haughty and impatient, was already making both friends and enemies. He knew the importance of speed in warfare. He wanted a swift attack on London.

There were those who agreed with him. The defenses of London were not ready, they said. Now was the time to strike.

But others were against it. Like true Englishmen they shirked doing the things that war made necessary. They advised caution.

Some were plainly jealous of Rupert. They listened to him with impatience. It was all very well for a foreigner to talk, but this was England, not Germany. The citizens of London would not surrender without a blow. It was better to collect more men first.

The king listened to all. His mind was swayed this way and that. At last he tried to please everybody. He decided that he would advance on London, but not too quickly.

His army went by way of Banbury, Oxford and Abingdon along deep-rutted, miry roads that were golden with the litter of autumn trees. The drums sounded hollowly across wide and hedgeless fields where laborers in country smocks straightened their backs from toil and came running to see the banners pass.

Sometimes the brave glitter of pikes lightened a landscape still somber with the shaggy remnants of ancient forests. Here and there a manor house shone pale amid its parkland. But there was little else, for England was still a country of scattered hamlets and tiny market towns.

In all of those he visited, Charles was greeted with joy. The people's sudden loyalty was displayed in speeches of welcome and the gift of embroidered banners. Without meeting any resistance the king reached Windsor on November 9th.

Two days before that, the Earl of Essex had entered London with his somewhat puzzled army. The citizens learned at first hand what had happened at Edgehill. The earl made the best tale he could, but it was not encouraging.

One thing was plain. The king was on his way with a big army. A peace party began to make its voice heard.

It was now, however, that ordinary folk began to show their quality. Out from the shops and warehouses poured the young men and maidens of London Town. Together they toiled on hasty earthworks and piled-up barricades, while their elders brought a steady procession of suitable refreshment for the workers.

Within the city the trained bands mustered their strength. Guns were taken off the ships in the Thames and dragged by teams of horses westward. The poet Milton sat down and wrote a poem which he stuck to his front door. It appealed to the invader to spare his humble home.

So each in his own way prepared his defense, while in Parliament a great argument raged. Pym and Hampden were together on one side against the fainthearts on the other. To soothe their opponents and to gain time they began to treat with the king.

But all the time Pym's shrewd brain was at work, while John Hampden, with his honest smile and friendly manner, won over some of the waverers. They listened to Pym and they trusted Hampden.

They knew, too, that they could not trust the king; not with power, at any rate. If he entered London in triumph there would soon be an end to Parliament.

They quickly discovered that Charles demanded nothing less. He saw himself as the victor and he asked for too much. Presently he became impatient.

On November 12th he unleashed Prince Rupert. The cavalry galloped toward Brentford and took it by storm. In the smoke of burning houses all thought of peace was smothered. Men who had lost their all came running to London with tales of what this German princeling would do.

The king's main army advanced through the blackened ruins of Brentford. The young man, M.S., who
had run away from his home in Cheshire, was with it.
He was probably seeing the south country for the first
time. But, by his own account, he was an unwelcome
visitor. He wrote as follows:

> Unexpectedly we were encountered by two or three
> regiments of theirs who had made some small barri-
> cades. . . . The van of our army, being about a thou-
> sand musketeers, answered their shot so bitterly that
> within an hour or less, they forsook that place and
> fled up to another . . . from whence and from a brick
> house nearby they gave us a hot and long shower of
> bullets.

There was now no flinching on either side. M.S. was
in the sixth regiment to be thrown into the attack. They
fired and charged and gained the day.

But M.S. was sorrowful in spite of the victory. It was,
he wrote, "heartbreaking to see the miserable deaths of
so many goodly men."

The next morning brought a novelty in warfare — an
inland naval action. Fourteen barges were wending their
slow way up the river from Kingston to London. Their
decks were encumbered with thirteen pieces of ordnance
and six hundred men. They had probably been hoping
to make the passage in darkness.

Suddenly, Royalist fire burst upon them from Sion
House. Bullets and cannonballs threshed the quiet waters of the Thames to foam. Five barges were sunk and

the rest were captured, according to M.S., "with three pieces in them for breakfast."

Meanwhile the advanced forces under Rupert had reached Turnham Green. He found the Earl of Essex facing him with twice his numbers and a battle front bristling with the cannons that had been hauled from London.

The prince had already learned something of the courage of English foot soldiers. He must have known that those massed thousands of musketeers and pikemen would not easily be broken. Behind them was the hostile city, with its silver pathway of river stretching to the sea.

Up that bright pathway could come men and supplies from every corner of England. The guns of the fleet had it in their charge, and the fleet was the servant of Parliament.

How much of this was in Rupert's mind we cannot know. But while he paused, the guns of the enemy thundered. In the battle smoke of the rebel line the king's advance was checked. His first chance of winning the war had gone.

M.S. may have heard those guns but he never saw them. He advanced no farther than Sion House. On the next day, he tells us, they withdrew to Kingston in the face of a great army coming from London.

We hear little more from him after that. Let us hope that the brave and generous M.S. survived the war and lived long. England was to need such men in the years to come.

The great army from which he retreated certainly did

not chase him far. The Earl of Essex, still bent on avoiding defeat, led it as far as Windsor. There he rested comfortably to see the winter through.

The king retired to Oxford and set to fortifying it. Strong positions were created at outlying towns to cover its approaches.

For the next three years Oxford was to be the capital of Charles's shifting military kingdom. Here, amid its ancient colleges, was set the scene of jealousy and intrigue in which one courtier strove with another for the favor of the king. The fickle brilliance of his court cast many a dark shadow. It was at Oxford that the war was to be lost.

It was not being lost in the north and west. There, even in the depth of winter, the king's friends were active. Elsewhere, too, were local skirmishes, with old neighbors paying off long-standing grudges and with new hatreds being born from violence and injustice.

Ralph Hodgson of Coley Hall, near Halifax, gives us his picture of the times. He tells how Sir William Saville came with horse, foot and two great guns on the Sabbath morning against Bradford Church, where the Roundhead townsfolk had fled for shelter.

A messenger came speeding from Bradford. He reached Halifax Vicarage and gasped out his news. A man called Isaac Baume ran to tell the minister, Mr. Latham, what was afoot. Mr. Latham roused his congregation from their enjoyment of his sermon.

They followed him, full of fight, to Bradford, where

they set upon the enemy with clubs and scythes tied to poles. These homemade weapons drove off the soldiers but failed to capture Sir William Saville's guns.

The affray, however, had one important result for Ralph Hodgson.

"I was resolved to stay by it," he tells us, and gives his reasons. "The king at his coronation swears to rule his people according to the law." He suspected, too, that "there was a Popish party about the king."

So Hodgson, afterward a captain, drew his sword for Parliament and, after much fighting, lived to see the end of it all.

In 1642 nobody could see the end of it, not even Oliver Cromwell. He was busy organizing the eastern counties into an association for carrying on the war. At that time few people except his friends and neighbors had ever heard of him, but he was very popular in his own county.

A plain Huntingdon squire with a somewhat untidy appearance — that was Cromwell in the years before the war. He had helped some of his poorer neighbors in a legal matter which had threatened their livelihoods and had been elected a Member of Parliament.

There were better talkers than himself at Westminster, but he knew and trusted the ordinary simple people more than they did. When men went from talking to doing, Cromwell came into his own.

His complete faith in God, his great energy and his

rough-and-ready manner soon made his presence felt all over East Anglia.

That part of the country was staunch for Parliament, and Cromwell was determined to keep it so. There was a growing threat from Yorkshire in the north. In order to meet it, Cromwell was busy recruiting men, picking them carefully and rejecting the ne'er-do-wells who were merely searching for plunder and were too easily come by.

Meanwhile, at Oxford and London, that winter was a season for hard thinking and careful planning. It was clear now that the war could not be won at a single blow. Everything was needed for the campaigns of the year to come.

Horses and men were the least of the problems. There was also food and shelter wanted for both. Weapons of all kinds were needed. That meant the cutting of timber to feed the furnaces that would smelt the iron. Charcoal, too, must be burned and powdered. It was wanted for mixing with saltpeter and other things, to make gunpowder.

Lead guttering and piping was being melted down for casting into bullets. Leather by the ton was required for boots and saddles and winter coats.

The merchants of London, skilled in trade, rubbed their hands together and began to furnish what was needed. But the men at Oxford were only a little way behind. They had been brought up to manage great

estates in a time when even villages were self-support-
ing. They knew their business almost as well as any
merchant.

So the strength of both sides grew. Their power to
hurt each other increased.

IV

The Weapons

Both sides now needed money to carry on the war. The wealthy merchants responded to Parliament's appeal by lending vast sums at a good rate of interest. The king had to rely on gifts from his supporters.

There was no stinting of these, but they were not always easy to convey to the king. In those days there were no banks in which cash could be held. A man paid his bills out of a money chest kept in his own house.

Rich people kept their savings in the form of gold and silver plate. If they needed large sums quickly they could sell it or pledge it at a goldsmith's, where money-lending was often practiced as a sideline.

It was this cumbersome treasure which now had to be taken to the king across country which was often in enemy hands. One of the Cambridge colleges which tried to send Charles its plate was surprised by Oliver Cromwell and forced to disgorge before the treasure was dispatched.

There were other such accidents, but the loyal Cavaliers managed to keep the rich stream flowing. Not sparing themselves, they did not spare their enemies. Plunder by both sides became common.

A complaint from Kent states:

In October last he was demanded by Sir John Sedley . . . what armes, horse money or plate he would lend or give to Parliament. He answered, his horse, armes and ammunition was already taken away for Parliament's service, that he had many other goods taken away and his house then set on fire.

The victim in this case was told that it had all been a mistake; but there were nine more such mistakes to follow. He complained that he was robbed "ten several times."

It was Parliament men who had plundered him, although at the same time they were complaining bitterly about what Rupert was doing. The prince was busily earning himself a new nickname. His enemies were beginning to mock him as the Duke of Plunderland.

The money thus raised by both sides was spent freely. At Oxford and London thousands of musketeers and pikemen were being hastily drilled. It was, however, only the biggest and strongest men who were chosen to "trail the pike."

It was sixteen feet long and needed plenty of muscle to control it. There was more than a chance of poking out some comrade's eye if the pikeman happened to be clumsy, and he had everything to make him so.

Besides his pike, he carried also a sword of poor quality to protect himself in a scrimmage at really close quarters when the unwieldy pike would be useless. Most of his safety, however, came from his body armor. It consisted of a heavy iron corselet and an iron helmet.

There is much of this equipment in museums today. Where you can see armor, look closely to detect a small round dent in it. This is the mark of the proofing bullet which was always fired at a newly made "back and breast" to ensure that it was tough enough to safeguard its owner's life.

One can see, too, the kind of bullet that made the dent. It was a round ball of lead, weighing twelve to the pound. When lead was scarce, however, these bullets were sometimes made smaller.

The musketeer could make them himself in the bullet mold he carried. He kept bullets in a leather pouch, but when battle was at hand he clapped two or three into his mouth, where they were handy.

He had many complicated things to do before he fired them. The charges had to be made up from his powder horn. This he did in advance and hung the charges, wrapped in paper, on a bandolier which he slung around his neck.

The rattling of these charges in the wind sometimes gave him away during a night attack. But his hands were too busy at other tasks for him to stop the noise.

He had to drop both charge and bullet down the four-foot length of his barrel and then ram them tight with a gunstick. He had to fill the pan of his musket with powder and then make sure that the wind did not blow it away before he was ready to press his *tricker*.

He could not, of course, keep such a long-barreled weapon steady on his target, so he had to support it on a stand which he carried with him and thrust into the ground before firing.

Added to all this, he had several yards of slow match wound around his waist and had to hold its burning end delicately between his fingers. One wonders how he ever fired at all.

The musketeer wore no armor, and relied on his legs to carry him to safety when he was charged. That safety he found behind hedges when he could; but hedges were still scarce in many parts of the kingdom, so when he was hard pressed he would scurry between the ranks of the pikemen. They were usually better than hedges, being solid with armor and bristling with steel.

An attack on such troops by cavalry was like a fight between a dog and a hedgehog. Courage and determination meant everything.

The horseman was armored on his back and breast and he also wore a helmet, but there were plenty of places where he could be hit by the musketeer or stabbed by the pikeman. The pike, moreover, bore a hook which could be used to drag an unlucky rider from the saddle.

The cavalry carried good swords, heavy pistols and sometimes carbines. Quite often they had poleaxes as well. They could ride up and exchange shots with the enemy, but this would not win battles. Only when the horse charged home could the solid mass of pikemen be broken. At such times the leading horse would suffer, but once the foot were scattered they became an easy prey for the speeding riders.

Cannons were also used to break up enemy forces, but were not very effective at the beginning. As the war went on they became bigger, but all except the very smallest were hard to move.

Nor were the gunners allowed to fire with impunity. Dragoons, who were mounted infantry, would ride up and dismount to pour in fire at close quarters. They used a better, flintlock musket which had once been called a *dragon,* and it was this weapon which earned the dragoons their name.

Such warfare as this was deadly. Perhaps deadlier still were the doctors and surgeons who tended the wounded. They were ignorant of germs and of the human body. They used magical preparations instead of proper medicines and they were forced to do dreadful operations without anesthetics.

In spite of all these terrors, however, and in spite of all other hardships, men came forward by the thousands to fight for what they believed in.

A Roundhead, writing in April 1643, gives us some idea of their spirit. He signed the initials T.C. to this letter. "I thanke my God I find as much comfort and health lying under a hedge and suffering Hunger, Thirst and Cold as when I lay on a feather bed and fared well."

Such men as he were now finding other uses for feather beds. There were no spring mattresses in the England of those days. The poor lay on pallets of straw, but the well-to-do handed down their warm feather beds from generation to generation. They were supported on dozens of cords stretched between the uprights at head and foot, and were very comfortable.

The cords, however, could be used at a pinch to make slow match for soldiers' muskets. This match was always scarce because it had to be kept burning when enemy forces were about. So many a sleepy citizen suddenly found himself dumped rudely on the floor by musketeers who happened to be fighting in the neighborhood.

It happened often enough in the year 1643, for during the previous winter the land had been sprouting armed men. Many were volunteers, but others were pressed into service whether they liked it or not.

By the ancient laws of the kingdom, able-bodied men over the age of sixteen could be compelled to serve as foot soldiers. Men of higher estate had to provide armed horsemen. The trouble, however, was that the pressed men would run away home at the first opportunity.

This is why we find that during the war armies seemed to spring up as if by magic and vanish again with equal suddenness at the first sign of defeat. Both king and Parliament preferred volunteers.

The pressed men were needed all the same. Sir Samuel Luke, that little fire-eater whom we last met trying to arrest Sir Lewis Dyve, tried his hand at forcible recruiting in the summer of 1643. He posted the following notice:

> ... If all persons in every parish betwixt sixteen and sixty, being able to carry arms, shall not severally appear at Laighton on Monday morning next by seven of the clock with all provisions and Arms and Weapons, he will proceed against such cold and insensible persons with that rigor and severitie as is done in other places.

It sounds like a cheerful start to somebody's week, and we can imagine the amount of grumbling and sudden illness which doubtless broke out in Laighton on Sunday. But in July 1643 Sir Samuel Luke had some excuse for his "severitie." Things were looking very black for Parliament.

The Earl of Essex had wasted the winter months at

SIR THOMAS FAIRFAX

Windsor but his enemies had not. In the north and west the Royalists had been active.

The king's northern commander, the Earl of Newcastle, had driven the Roundheads away from York. Lord Fairfax, the Roundhead leader, was forced to retire to Selby, leaving the Yorkshire weaving towns open to attack.

Those little towns held out stubbornly, and were presently relieved by Fairfax's son, Sir Thomas Fairfax, who had a knack of being on hand when he was needed. But the Royalists, in far greater force, were pressing confidently southward.

In Cornwall also there had been great victories for the king. At Stratton in the month of May, the Cornishmen under Sir Ralph Hopton trapped a Roundhead force which had rashly ventured from Devon. Without cannons and against odds of two to one, the Cornishmen stormed up Stamford Hill.

They killed or captured two thousand of the enemy and seized a great store of arms. With added strength they crossed the county border and quickly overran the rich Devon countryside. The Roundheads in Plymouth shut their gates and prepared for siege.

Truly, as somebody said, "The common people addicted to the King's service have come out of blind Wales and other dark corners of the land."

The dark corner of Cornwall was bright with glory as Hopton led his men eastward. He was on his way to fulfill his share of the king's new war plan.

His task was to battle through the southern counties until he reached the Thames below London. This war, fought by armies upon an island, depended on the sea. The king knew that London must be sealed off from the ships that gave her strength.

In May 1643, however, Sir Ralph had far to go. Another Parliamentary army was marching through the west. It was led by a prim professional soldier, Sir William Waller, who happened to be a great friend of Hopton's.

They exchanged letters full of noble feeling. Waller said that they were like actors on a stage. They must play their parts until the tragedy was ended.

Far different were the letters that Waller exchanged with his ally, the Earl of Essex. These two Roundhead leaders were bitterly jealous of each other. Neither would ever help the other if he could avoid it.

It was not long before Waller found himself cut off from London and was asking Essex for aid. The earl, however, had other plans. With great skill Waller brought his army to Lansdown Hill, near Bath, and strongly fortified it.

From any ordinary enemy he would have had little to fear. But he had not met Hopton's Cornishmen or their like before.

Attack after attack was launched up the precipitous slopes. Time after time the Cornish were beaten back from a summit ringed with Waller's roaring guns. But at dusk they had gained the crest and were facing the rest of the Roundhead army.

The enemy stood their ground. The night came down on a scene of fire and fury. Then Waller ordered his still-unbroken forces to retreat.

"We were glad they were gone," reported a Royalist. "For if they had not, I know who had, within the hour."

So ended the Battle of Lansdown, with both armies exhausted. Waller had served Parliament well. His army was still in the field. While it was unbroken, the king's new war plan could never work.

It was, however, a very good plan on paper. Charles meant to keep his main army near Oxford and threaten London from there. This, he hoped, would pin down the Earl of Essex at Windsor.

Meanwhile, Hopton was to advance from the southwest and the Earl of Newcastle would march from the north. The plan was for these two to join hands across the Thames at a point below London.

When that had been done, Charles would launch his main attack from Oxford. With London isolated, the head of the rebellion would be neatly cut off.

It was a complicated plan but, for a time, it looked like succeeding. The snag, in the early summer of 1643, was Waller's army.

He had begun a counterattack on Hopton. The Cornish were weakened by their losses at Lansdown and were soon in danger. Hopton had been injured by an exploding powder wagon and was too weak to leave his bed.

But he used his sickroom as a headquarters and fought desperately back against Waller's attack. His plight moved the king to action, and his courage soon had its reward.

A strong force of cavalry swept out of Oxford toward Bristol. It was led by Prince Maurice, Rupert's younger brother. At Roundway Down, near Bristol, he overwhelmed Waller and practically destroyed his army.

The triumphant Cavaliers swept on to Bristol, which yielded almost at once. Soon they were overrunning the rolling downs of Dorset. A great city and another county had been won.

Elsewhere in England, away from the main battlefields, the dingdong struggle was continuing. Towns and manor houses were captured and recaptured. Local quarrels flamed fiercely and old scores were paid off.

But the stronger tides of war seemed to be setting against Parliament. In the north, the Fairfaxes had come to grief at Adwalton Moor. Now, in the whole kingdom, three cities only were holding up the king's attack on London.

Hull was still untaken, so was Gloucester and so was Plymouth. The fate of England rested on the courage of their citizens. Without Hull in their hands, the men of Yorkshire dared not advance south. Until Gloucester was taken, the hardy Welsh would not risk crossing the Severn. Only when Plymouth fell could Hopton use his full force in the south.

But Charles had Bristol. It was all the more a prize because the seas no longer belonged to Parliament alone. Dozens of privateers were now afloat in the king's cause. The seas were swarming with other small ships, out for all they could get. They were harrying the merchant shipping and keeping Parliament warships busy.

The king was hoping for fresh troops from Ireland. It was a hope nourished in his mind by Queen Henrietta Maria. She had managed at last to cross stormy seas and reach England safely.

On the voyage her ship had nearly sunk. Her frightened ladies had gathered around her for comfort. "Queens of England never drown," she had told them gaily.

Now she added her voice to the babble of counsel which was bewildering the king. She was joyful at the news out of Ireland. A Roman Catholic revolt was flooding to success there. The rebels had formed their own government and had even struck a seal for the passing of their new laws. The seal bore the motto: IRISHMEN UNITED FOR GOD, KING AND COUNTRY.

But success in Ireland was doing Charles more harm than good. The hatred and fear that Englishmen felt for the Irish is unbelievable to us today. An Irishman taken in battle was killed out of hand. Even an Irishwoman might be treated in the same way.

So the news brought Parliament more support than ever. Men who had hesitated now became sure that Charles and his Catholic wife meant to force Popery on them.

For men like these there was one bright gleam amid the darkening prospect of the war. In May 1643 there had been a skirmish at Belton, just north of Grantham, in Lincolnshire.

Twelve troops of Roundhead horse had routed twice that number of Cavaliers. The victors were men who "knew what they were fighting for and loved what they knew."

They were led by the man who had chosen them and trained them. He was Colonel Oliver Cromwell.

V

High Tide

The swinging swords and steady horse which had won Cromwell's small victory at Belton were taking part in the muddled fighting that was going on in Lincolnshire.

Farther north, in Yorkshire, Sir Thomas Fairfax was still in the field for Parliament, but making no headway. Meanwhile, Prince Rupert was creating havoc in the south with widespread raids on Roundhead convoys and outposts.

On June 17th he struck out from Oxford with eighteen hundred men. Under cover of darkness his men advanced swiftly through enemy country.

He was searching for a treasure chest which was on its way with money to pay Roundhead troops. The wagoners were warned of his coming and took refuge in the woods until the danger was past.

Rupert missed the money, but scattered an unlucky garrison at Stokenchurch and then rode on to Chinnor. In the gray light of dawn his men burst in on the enemy, killing many and spreading alarm throughout the countryside. Then Rupert fell back toward Oxford.

But the enemy had rallied and were soon at his heels. They caught up with him at Chalgrove Field just as he was about to cross a river. Led by such brave fighters as Sir Samuel Luke and John Hampden, they lined the hedges with musketeers and began to pepper him hotly.

"This insolence is not to be borne!" declared the haughty Rupert.

His Cavaliers turned to charge. They gained the hedge and began to drive the musketeers from their leafy shelters. Up came Hampden with support for his infantry, and a general scrimmage ensued.

By the time the fight was over, John Hampden had fallen with a wound that proved mortal. He lingered a week or so before yielding up his brave spirit in the cause he had served so well.

His death spread gloom in London. Even in the enemy ranks there were many who grieved for him. He had been foremost in the struggle against the king, but all his actions had been guided by honor and courage. Now he was gone, and England was the worse for it. The war seemed to be devouring all that was best in the land.

His friend John Pym must have felt it most of all. Pym, too, was dying, but not by the hand of man. Racked with pain from an internal disease, he sat at council after council and forced his tired brain to complete the work it had so shrewdly begun.

The plans he had laid were bearing ugly fruit. It was Pym who had led the opposition to Charles. It was Pym who had brought the Earl of Strafford to the executioner's block. He had framed the Grand Remonstrance which had stripped Charles of nearly all his powers except that of the armed forces. His attempt to take even that had forced the king to fight.

Until then all had gone well. Now, with defeat in three corners of the kingdom, there were fainthearts in London who were advising surrender.

Pym strove with them day and night, pleading and arguing and threatening. His dying eyes were still able to see further and more clearly than most men's. Gradually he brought the others to realize where the key to victory lay.

Slowly, painfully, he hammered out a treaty with the Scots. He yielded much and promised much to bring their troops over the border.

In return for Scottish help, Parliament would pay £100,000 cash down and £30,000 a month thereafter. Besides this, the English Church would be altered to the Scottish pattern. Bishops were to be abolished and the English Parliament would take the oath of the Scottish Covenant.

Before the treaty was signed, however, the war had taken a new turn. A young man of twenty-three had brought all the king's victories to naught. His name was Edward Massey and he was the colonel in command of the garrison at Gloucester.

He somehow misled Charles into believing that he was ready to give up the city. Instead of marching on London, the king decided that he would collect this easy prize first. He appeared outside Gloucester on August 10th and confidently demanded its surrender.

He received a rude surprise. Out from the city gate stalked two men, a soldier and a citizen. They bared their heads and faced the king boldly. He could have Gloucester, they said, when orders came from Parliament, but not before. Then they turned on their heels, replaced their hats and strode calmly back to their friends.

The courtiers tittered at their quaint appearance but the king was angry at the rebuff he had received. Gloucester must be taught a lesson, he decided. The siege of the city began.

The Royalists at once mounted a fierce attack. Forcing their way into the city outskirts, they set a church ablaze and burned down many houses. But the flames they had kindled drove them back. In the time gained, the citizens threw up more barricades.

For several more days the fighting went on, but the

Royalists made little headway. The men of Gloucester were battling for their homes and families. They had heard tales of what the Cavaliers would do, and they had a leader they could trust.

The young governor, Edward Massey, was everywhere, heartening the defenders and directing the struggle. He had earth piled up behind the walls to strengthen them. He spread his forces to protect every point and, when the Royalists cut the water supplies, he had water pumped out of the Severn to take their place.

Meanwhile the king's engineers were digging mines beneath the gates. The Royalist gunners were keeping up a steady battering of the walls. As the stonework weakened, the women and children of Gloucester toiled to repair the damage. Under enemy fire they carried baskets of earth to fill up the holes. When earth could not be brought, they used precious woolpacks or bedding or anything else that was handy.

But Gloucester did not rely only on defense. Small parties of men struck back in spirited sallies which tried to spike the enemy guns and drove the attackers from their nearest outposts.

If courage alone were needed, then Gloucester would never fall. But soon supplies began to run short. Anxiously the defenders looked from their walls and scanned the eastern hills for signs of approaching help.

They saw little to comfort them. The Royalists were ravaging the surrounding countryside. The sun gleamed on the steel of enemy horsemen riding the distant slopes. The king's troops seemed to be everywhere.

Mocking messages, tied to arrows, sped over the walls. They told the citizens that all their friends had been defeated. The Earl of Essex was far away in London and dared not come, wrote the Royalists. Why not surrender and save their own lives?

On August 24th the city had a narrow escape. Heavy rain fell just as Charles was preparing to explode his mines. The tunnels were flooded and the engineers were forced, drenched and gasping, to leave their work. The city gained a little more time.

In London, meanwhile, John Pym was straining every nerve and sinew to raise men and supplies for the Earl of Essex. On August 26th the Roundhead army set out for Aylesbury. From there it moved past Oxford, harassed continually by Royalist cavalry. Doggedly it marched onward to Gloucester.

There, the struggle for the city was continuing. Redhot cannonballs were being used to try to fire the houses. Day and night the citizens and soldiers shared the dangers of the walls. There were too few of them to give each other rest. They had to snatch sleep when and where they could.

Their powder was running low. The great enemy assault would come as soon as the powder was gone. Yet they were determined never to surrender.

At last, wrote one of them, "we discerned two fires upon Wainload Hill." It was the signal that help was on its way, and it was coming only just in time. Colonel Massey was down to his last three barrels of gunpowder.

On September 5, 1643, a night of wind and rain, the Earl of Essex came in sight of Gloucester. He had no battle to fight, because Charles was already in retreat, afraid to risk his cavalry amid the hedgerows of the surrounding countryside.

The siege of Gloucester was over. It was proof that the citizens of England, and their wives and children too, could fight as bravely as any gentleman-at-arms. What had been done at Gloucester was done also at Plymouth and at Hull and at a score of other towns up and down the land.

Now, in September 1643, the Earl of Essex had to find his way back to London. His was the only army Parliament had to protect the capital. The other one was being hard pressed in the northeast. If Charles could destroy Essex, the failure at Gloucester would have been well worthwhile.

The earl realized his peril, and tried to throw Charles off the scent by pretending to march on Worcester. Then he doubled back toward Cirencester.

He was short of food and ammunition. Ahead of him lay a long march through a ravaged countryside menaced by a powerful enemy. His position seemed hopeless.

The lucky capture of a Royalist convoy gave him the chance to feed his men. He began a swift march toward Cricklade, hoping to dodge Charles on the way home.

Meanwhile Prince Rupert was searching frantically for his uncle and the main Royalist army, which seemed to have vanished. Just in time he found Charles, coolly playing cards and waiting for news.

The king at once gave the orders to march. His army tramped in pursuit of Essex, following a different route to head him off at Newbury.

But the earl was winning the race. Rupert's men, riding through drenching rain, met his vanguard at Aldbourne beneath the chalk hills of Wiltshire. In a sharp little action he checked the Roundheads and gave Charles time to bar the London road.

On the evening of September 19th the king's army ranged itself along a ridge just south of Newbury and awaited the earl's attack.

Attack he must, or starve where he stood. The weary Roundheads, hungry and soaked to the skin, lay in the fields below and waited for the dawn. Then, in the cool September morning, a savage battle began.

It was fought in a tangle of lanes and hedges that sloped steeply up to the ridge where the Royal Standard drooped damply above the smoke of cannons. From one little knoll to another, between blackberry bushes diamonded with rain, the sweating troops stumbled and struggled as the day wore on.

On their left the Roundheads gradually made headway, pressing the king's men back across ground that was taken and retaken again and again. But they were unable to break through.

On the right their danger was acute. It was open country there, with no friendly hedges to shield them from Rupert's splendid horsemen. The Roundhead cavalry was beaten off the field, and only two regiments of London trained bands were left to face the prince's onslaught.

Bravely the former apprentices and shopkeepers closed their ranks to meet his charge. Time and again Rupert attacked, pausing every now and then to batter them with cannon fire. But in spite of all he could do, the Londoners held their ranks firm.

Step by step they withdrew to safer ground. Then, with hedges around them, they did not give another inch.

All day long the battle lasted. Only when night came at last did the armies fall silent. Each had endured to the utmost. Neither could claim a victory.

Although the Royalists had been forced back across a few hundred yards of bloodstained ground they were still barring the road to London. The Roundhead attack had failed.

But during the night King Charles changed his mind. He, like Essex, had spent most of his ammunition and he was shaken by the slaughter of his friends. Among the rest, Viscount Falkland had fallen.

Falkland, one of the most noble of men, had loved his king and country in equal measure. At Gloucester he had prayed over and over again for peace. At Newbury, full of despair at what was happening to England, he had thrown his life away.

Alone, he had spurred his horse into a little lane lined with quickset hedges that ran rivers of fire from enemy muskets. It was certain death and he had known it, but he had lost the will to live.

Hundreds of others were dead when sunset came. In the darkness of night the haunted king marched his army away. When daylight dawned the weary soldiers of Parliament found the road to London open. The high tide of the king's victories was past.

In the north things were also going badly for the king. On September 22nd, two days after the fight at Newbury, Oliver Cromwell managed to reach Hull with fresh supplies of arms and powder for the garrison.

Having given what help he could, Cromwell returned with Sir Thomas Fairfax into Lincolnshire. There, at Winceby, they began a partnership of unbroken victory. Yet Winceby was nearly an end and not a beginning for Cromwell.

When his cavalry was trotting smartly forward to attack, a cannonball struck his horse and brought it headlong. Cromwell went down with it but managed to fall clear. As he scrambled to his feet he was knocked down again by one of his own troopers.

Undaunted, he jumped up again and found another horse. He plunged into the fight, Fairfax charged and the day was theirs. Three weeks later the Royalists raised the siege of Hull. On October 20th the Earl of Manchester captured Lincoln for Parliament.

Even King Charles must have realized that the tables were now turned. But war is full of surprises, and he still had a good army. People everywhere were growing weary of the war. By keeping in the field, by bringing London's inland trade to a standstill, Charles could still hope to force peace on his own terms.

As the autumn leaves fell in that second year of war he must have been heartened by the news from London.

John Pym was failing fast. On December 8, 1643, the king's greatest enemy passed away.

There was nobody to take the place of John Pym, nobody who could handle so skillfully the men inside Parliament and the London mob outside it.

New men must now try to govern England. There was always the chance that they would quarrel among themselves.

VI

The People

While all these great events were happening, the small daily actions of ordinary life had to continue.

The citizens of Gloucester had fought bravely for their homes. The London lads had stood like heroes at Newbury. Yet, most people in England wanted the war to end.

There was great suffering everywhere, even in places where the battles did not rage. In London, during the winter of 1643–44, there was almost no fuel. The city had begun to depend on coal shipped from Newcastle. This trade had been brought to a standstill.

To go through a winter without heat would be hardship enough for most of us today. In the seventeenth century it must have been far worse. The houses were draftier places and there were no carpets or curtains to take the chill from plaster walls or stone floors, except in the homes of the very richest people.

Moreover, the housewife was dependent on open fires for her cooking and breadmaking. Her kitchen was the very heart of the household.

When her family went out into the muddy winter streets they wore no raincoats to keep out the rain. A leather coat or jerkin would have to suffice. Ordinary working people were always short of clothing. They were worse off still, now that the woolen trade with the west country was cut off by Royalist raiding.

What clothes they did wear were probably warm enough, but there was little to change into when they came home drenched to the skin after the hard labor of a winter's day. A cold supper, washed down with chilly ale, must have been a cheerless affair without the brightness of flame dancing on the hearth.

Even a bed was something of a luxury. The whole of a man's furniture might be no more than a bench, a stool or two, a table and a few chests.

With the shutters fastened against the night, and a tallow candle shedding only enough radiance to make the shadows visible, a London home could have been a dreary place in January 1644.

If it was not, it was because of the strong faith and high spirits of the people themselves. They were not all Puritans, and even the Puritans knew how to be gay. There was plenty of music and singing in the ordinary household.

Nobody expected life to be easy. A man must earn his family's bread by the sweat of his brow. The Bible said that, and the Bible was God's word. It was enough to do one's duty and trust in Providence for all else.

So family prayers and readings were a nightly event. Everybody had a great interest in the tales of the Old and New Testaments. They expected God to take a hand in human affairs.

This was true throughout the land. In the country, however, some of the other ways of life might be different from what they were in towns.

There was little fear of going cold while trees grew in the woods. Nor was there always such need to be abroad throughout a winter's day.

Work on the farms could pause for really bad weather. It was always difficult to feed animals during the winter because of the seasonal shortage of fodder. So a great many were slaughtered every autumn, even in peacetime.

In bitter weather the laborer could thresh grain in the barn and even the shepherd could huddle in a shelter until the worst was past. But the countryman's life was balanced always between the richness of autumn and the hungry gap of spring.

In October there would be fruit and nuts aplenty,

grain in abundance and a farmyard full of fat cattle. Barns and storehouses were so crammed that even the poor might expect their share.

This time of good living might last through Christmas and beyond. By February, however, many of the goods in store would be past their best. A plentiful use of salt would have kept some of the meat from the autumn killings, but there would now be little of it left.

Everything would be scarce. Few hens would be laying, milk yields would be scanty, and all but the hardest cheeses would be threatened with mold. Only the shrewdest foresight on the part of the housewife could keep a family in health until the grass began to grow again.

Centuries of experience had taught countryfolk just how much they needed to tide them over. They had learned how many cattle their garnered hay could feed, how much butter must be salted down, what amount of bacon must be smoked and how much fruit must be dried or otherwise preserved.

To keep too much was almost as bad as keeping too little. It meant less to sell at the market and it put a strain on precious storage space. The countryman had to hold a balance between waste and want.

This balance in their lives was now rudely upset by throngs of armed men who came demanding this or that in the name of king or Parliament.

To the simple farmer both sides were robbers. He saw his barns emptied of grain and his haystack pulled down to feed other men's beasts. He was often ill-treated, his wife insulted and his children scared almost out of their wits.

Small wonder that he began to hate the brawny, leather-coated troopers who jingled away down the lane and left him to the bareness of his plundered homestead. In desperation, many of the countrymen began to band themselves together to resist both sides.

They raised armed bands which went by the name of Clubmen. These were especially numerous in the west of England, but they were too badly organized to achieve very much.

Nothing seemed to check the insolence of the soldiers. There were times when two parties of Royalists might fight each other for the right to plunder some particular district. If a local leader tried to be a little kinder, there was always some stranger to threaten him.

One Royalist commander wrote as follows to a community which had failed to meet his demands: "You can expect an unsanctified troop of horse among you, from whom if you hide yourselves, they shall fire your houses without mercy, hang up your bodies wherever they find them and scare your ghosts."

Wealthier men who tried to keep out of the war were similarly threatened. Prince Rupert wrote this to Sir Thomas Hanmer at Appley Castle:

Mr. Hanmer is to consider whether he will man and maintain Appley Castle himself or leave it to another or have it blown up. And if he choose to keep it himself and hereafter lose it to the Rebel Enemy, then the damage that shall accrue to the King in the recovery thereof shall be refunded out of his estate.

Poor Sir Thomas had three choices only. He could fight for the king, give up his home to a garrison of strangers or see it blown to pieces.

He would have fared no better with a Roundhead commander. Both sides were hard on any rich man who refused to support them. But the shrewd committeemen in London worked more carefully than the outspoken Rupert. They wore down the fainthearts with fines and taxes.

In the field, too, the Roundheads were less tempted than the Royalists to plunder people. They were better supplied with everything and did not have to rely so much on what they could pick up. Thus, as the war went on, they gradually gained more sympathy for their cause.

They had always had plenty of support in the towns, and it was in the towns that the king's war was being lost. Wherever Charles turned he seemed to be faced by doughty citizens with a natural gift for breaking other people's heads.

Prince Maurice wrote a savage letter about the town of Lyme Regis which he had failed to capture: "This villainous town of Lyme has destroyed more brave gentlemen and men of honor than has been lost in all the West."

His words could have been echoed by other Royalist leaders all over the country. The towns of the north were also producing their humble heroes. The Bolton men seem to have been especially valorous.

They beat off two fierce attacks in February 1643 and another in the following March. Of the last, an eyewitness tells us: "The Minister of the town prayed with a company of soldiers, most of them townsmen. The end of the prayer was the beginning of the fight. The enemy came on desperately . . . some of them leaped upon the works, where they found clublaw."

Having driven off the enemy, the triumphant Bolton men marched off to Wigan and rescued their comrades there. They were forced out of Wigan again, but soon afterward they put to flight a large force of Royalists.

"So let all Thine enemies perish, O God!" cried one man of Lancashire.

He was almost certainly a townsman if he was on the Roundhead side. Most of the country people were followers of the Earl of Derby, the greatest landowner in the county. Derby had called hundreds of his tenants to fight for Charles. He made war roughly, and it took courage to make a stand against his swarming forces.

But that courage was being found in the most unlikely places. With it came an increasing skill in war which was beginning to worry the leading men on both sides. Prince Maurice's "brave gentlemen and men of honor" were being beaten at their own game.

At the onset of the war the commanders had all been

gentlemen, and the generals had been noblemen. They were the natural war leaders of the kingdom, just as the barons and knights had been in the days of Richard the Lionheart.

Now, however, it was beginning to look as if Jack was as good as his master. The butcher, the baker and the candlestick maker were all handling pikes and muskets, and they did not run away when they were charged by their betters.

Colonel Oliver Cromwell spoke out frankly in favor of these ordinary men. He said, "I had rather have a plain russet-coated captain that knows what he fights for and loves what he knows, than that which is called a gentleman and is nothing else."

So he went on choosing his officers from those who could lead men in battle. He wanted soldiers with good characters and keen brains. When he found them he cared nothing for what their fathers had been.

This did not always please other people. When they criticized him, Cromwell answered sharply:

"Gentlemen, it may be it provoked some spirits to see such plain men made captains of horse. . . . Better plain men than none."

In the heat of the moment he may have said other things more dangerous. The Earl of Manchester, with whom he was serving, accused him of declaring that he hoped to live to see never a nobleman in England.

Whether he said it or not, one thing was certain. A good many Roundhead leaders were deciding that Oliver Cromwell was a man to be watched. His influence was growing steadily because of his luck in the field. It was a pity, thought some, that the more respectable leaders could not gain victories.

By December 1643, the generals had little to show for all the pains the country had endured. Waller had lost a whole army at Roundway Down and was blaming Essex for not having come to help him.

The Earl of Essex had saved himself at Newbury but that was about all. Only the Earl of Manchester had tasted real success, and that was in Lincolnshire, where he had Cromwell and Fairfax to thank for it.

In January 1644 there was hope of better things to come. Waller had been given the command of a new army. It had taken some time to collect it because many of the men who had fought under Essex refused point-blank to serve with Waller. At last, however, it was ready.

The work it had to do was plain before it. During the winter Sir Ralph Hopton had been as busy as ever for King Charles. He had pressed on through Hampshire and had reached Sussex, which was in those days the center of the iron industry.

There amid the thinning forests of the Weald the charcoal burners plied their smoky trade. They alone could produce the fuel to smelt the local iron ore. Only charcoal would in those days burn hot enough to melt the iron. Men had not learned how to use coal for this purpose.

The guns which had battered the Armada had been made in Sussex, in thriving little villages which look today as if they have never known anything except the joy of apple blossom and the steady gold of grain.

But in 1644 the furnaces were glowing, the hammers were booming and the axes were flashing in the clearings. The ironmasters were working apace to feed the armies which were hungry for their cannons.

If Hopton could seize all that industry it would be a heavy blow against Parliament. Aware of the danger, Waller moved swiftly against him.

He caught Hopton at Alton with the Royalist army too far scattered. It was a chance Waller was too good a general to miss. He put Hopton's horse to flight and captured a good many of his foot.

These men were not the Cornishmen whom Hopton had led a year previously. Half of the prisoners changed sides. With increased strength Waller marched on to capture Arundel.

Hopton, however, was not a man to give up easily. He made for Winchester and managed to pick up reinforcements. Turning on Waller, he trapped him near Alresford.

Waller was in a dangerous position and would have retreated if possible, but Hopton forced him into battle. Fierce fighting raged in and around Cheriton Wood. The Royalist horse muddled themselves into hopeless disorder and suffered heavily. The battle ended with the Royalists in retreat and the king's threat to Sussex ended for good.

In this campaign Charles lost another brave servant. Sir John Smith, who had been knighted for saving the king's standard at Edgehill, was fatally wounded on

March 29th. He died at Andover soon afterward.

He was thirty years of age and had lived longer than young William Holles who had been shot and temporarily blinded in his company at Edgehill. William had been killed at Newark a year earlier, when he was only twenty-two.

So the good men died, and England was the poorer for their passing, but still the war continued. In fact, it was getting worse.

The Scots were now taking a hand in it. They had crossed the Tweed in January and had begun to move steadily south. They were well equipped and well cared for.

Parliament was allowing each Scottish trooper a shilling daily, plus fourpence for straw and sixpence for his horse's fodder. That sixpence bought three English gallons of oats. A dragoon's horse, however, did not fare so well; it had only two gallons of oats and three-pennyworth of straw.

This was because the dragoon was not expected to charge with the cavalry. His horse was a mere conveyance to carry him to the place where he fought on foot. It was now carrying him south into Yorkshire.

The two Fairfaxes were on the move north to meet their new allies. They stormed Selby and joined with the Scots at Tadcaster. At this news, the Earl of Newcastle, who was commanding for King Charles, fled away and shut himself up in York. The Scots and the Roundheads prepared to besiege the city.

It was now that quarrels began on both sides. Charles

had decided to build up his army at Oxford and began to recall the troops from elsewhere. He sent for Rupert to return from the north. The prince rode back to his uncle and presented himself, ready for argument.

He wanted Oxford held by a ring of strong garrisons. If this were done, he promised the king he would clear the north while his brother Maurice took a firm hold on the southwest.

The king listened to all Rupert had to say. Then he agreed. But as soon as the prince had returned happily to his command in the north, the king listened to other people. He began to call back the men from the outer garrisons.

He hoped in this way to create a strong army which by moving quickly in any direction from Oxford might hope to score a great victory. It was not a bad plan, but it gave Essex and Waller their chance.

One by one the king's undefended strongholds at Reading, Abingdon and Malmesbury fell to the advancing enemy. Essex and Waller began to close in on Oxford.

Then they quarreled! The king was showing unexpected signs of being a good general. He was keeping them both on the move and avoiding battle. He wrote to Rupert and promised to "spin out time" until the prince had relieved York.

He was spinning out the time so well that Essex became discouraged. The earl's only glory so far had come from his relief of Gloucester. He now wanted to repeat his exploit by marching off to relieve Lyme, still besieged by Maurice.

Waller, who was no fool, argued strongly against the plan. It did not matter whether Lyme was rescued or not. Charles must be captured before the war could end.

"Break his army never so often," he told Essex, "his person will raise another."

But Essex would not listen. He marched away and refused to turn back even when the men in London ordered him to do so. On he trailed into Dorset, where he relieved Lyme and occupied Weymouth.

Then, for all the world as if he had never clapped eyes on a map of England, he led his army into the narrowing Cornish peninsula. The men of Cornwall rose against him and he soon found himself in trouble.

Meanwhile, Waller had been checked by Charles at Cropredy Bridge, where a muddled and straggling battle had been fought across the lush green meadows on either side of the River Cherwell.

The battle left Charles free to move in any direction he liked.

VII

The New Model Army

Whiile Charles and Waller were dodging each other in the Midlands and while the Earl of Essex was plodding off into the southwest, Rupert was overrunning Lancashire.

Stockport fell and Bolton was stormed. At Bolton, the prince behaved with unusual savagery and massacred most of the garrison. He took Liverpool, then a small place, and began to recruit the Catholics of Lancashire, who came flocking to his triumphant banners.

In the hour of his success he received a fateful letter

from the king. It was the one in which Charles had promised to spin out time until Rupert had raised the siege of York.

The prince read it and took it as an order to relieve York at once. The Earl of Newcastle, who was defending the city, had begun to show signs of surrendering.

Rupert must have known that he was greatly outnumbered by the forces of Fairfax and his Scottish allies, but without awaiting reinforcements he rode for York at top speed.

His impetuous advance and his warlike fame led the enemy to retreat. Giving orders for the Royalists in York to follow him as soon as possible, the prince pressed on after Fairfax.

He caught the rearguard and brought it to a halt. Fairfax and the Scots turned back to assist the laggards and found themselves facing battle at Marston Moor.

For the first time in the war the two greatest cavalry leaders were to match their wits and courage.

"Is Cromwell there?" asked Rupert, splendid in a red cloak, as he questioned a captive. "Will they fight? If so, they shall have fighting enough."

"If it pleases God, so shall he," was Cromwell's grim reply when he received Rupert's message.

He had good reason for his confidence. The Scots and Roundheads were in far greater strength than the Royalists. They were troops of good quality, too, with fine commanders. Above all, Cromwell was certain that God was on his side.

In the early afternoon of July 2, 1644, the Scottish

and English foot were massed upon a ridge amid ripening rye fields. Slightly below them lay the open moor on which Rupert was waiting.

The garrison from York had not yet arrived. Not until four o'clock did the last tired troops reach the field after a seven-mile march. In the interval the prince had had plenty of time to survey the country.

In spite of this he rashly brought his men so close to the enemy that they were separated only by a ditch packed with Royalist musketeers. Then both armies waited while the afternoon slowly turned to evening.

At seven o'clock, when the summer shadows were lengthening, Rupert decided that there would be no battle that day. There were only two hours of daylight left.

Calmly he went off to his supper, while the Earl of Newcastle, who was commanding the Royalist foot, went off to his coach for a peaceful and comfortable smoke.

He was still filling his pipe when Cromwell charged across the ditch.

The surprise attack drove back Rupert's first regiment but did not break it. Rupert came galloping up to take command and quickly rallied his men. They began to fight back hard. It was Cromwell's turn to be in danger.

At the crisis of the struggle, the Scots came to his rescue. Their horse was led by little, crooked David Leslie, a cunning general with years of experience.

He avoided a head-on collision with Rupert and wheeled his men out to the left. Then he turned and crashed down on the prince's flank.

A long and fierce struggle followed. It ended with Rupert's fine cavalry being beaten off the field for the first time in the war.

But the battle was far from won. All this had taken place on the Roundhead left. Their right was in dire trouble. Here, Sir Thomas Fairfax had been charged by the Royalists under Goring, a brave and brutal man who could handle cavalry as well as anybody when hard knocks were being exchanged. Fairfax's cavalry fled before him.

In the center a dour struggle was going on. The two armies of infantry had collided in midfield and were now pushing and heaving against each other, stabbing at faces seen briefly through the smoke, clubbing their muskets and lunging with their pikes while the cannons thundered in their ears.

Sir Thomas Fairfax, with blood streaming from a face wound, rode around behind the swaying infantry and sought Cromwell through the murk of battle. Everything was now hanging in the balance.

The Roundhead reserve of foot had been broken by Goring's hard-riding Cavaliers. There was nothing else to throw into the fight. But Goring had gone on to attack the Roundhead supply wagons.

It was Edgehill repeated, with no Royalist horse on the field. The Cavaliers had made the same mistake again. This time, however, there was no second chance. In war, men must learn or perish! Cromwell had learned.

His disciplined troopers, earning that day from Rupert himself the proud title of Ironsides, were still under their leader's control. Cromwell led them across the field.

He arrived just in time to catch Goring's disordered riders coming back from their mission of plunder. A strong attack, driven home, sent them flying. The battle was won.

It was won, but not yet over. The white-coated infantry of the north were standing firm for King Charles amid the disaster. Outnumbered by the enemy foot and ringed around by hostile cavalry, they stubbornly refused to surrender.

Still fighting, they were gradually herded into a little enclosure where they died almost to a man. The victory was complete.

"God made them as stubble to our swords," declared the exulting Cromwell.

He had the grace to mention that there were "a few Scots in our rear," but he made it quite clear that it was God and Cromwell's Ironsides, working together, who had won the day.

The real truth was that, without David Leslie and his Scots, Cromwell might well have been a beaten man that night.

On the Royalist side everybody was blaming everybody else.

"I will not endure the laughter of the court," said the haughty Earl of Newcastle before he took a ship for Europe.

His men lay dead on the field of Marston Moor as he fled from the courtiers' smiles. The king's cause in the north was broken and there was no further attempt to hold York.

Rupert gathered six thousand of his scattered cavalry and rode south. He and the king between them still had a powerful force. Much might yet be done.

In London there was every cause for joy. It was the greatest victory either side had won since the war began. Surely, thought the citizens, the king must now seek a peace. Another winter of hardship might be avoided.

But Charles was not the man to give up trying. He too could deal heavy blows. He raced after the luckless Earl of Essex and closed the Cornish trap, herding the Roundheads into Lostwithiel and capturing nearly all of them.

Essex himself managed to escape by ship and returned to London to find himself even more unpopular than before. His defeat had dimmed the glory of Marston Moor; his desertion of his army had dimmed his own.

Both sides had now lost an army in the field. The game seemed to be even. But Parliament had other and worse troubles to face.

It was gradually becoming clear that men like Essex

did not wish to beat the king outright. They were fearful of the new men who were rising to command on their own side. They dreaded complete victory almost as much as they dreaded defeat.

They were still hoping to patch up a peace, and they had strong support in Parliament. If they had been dealing with any king except Charles they might have had their way. But Charles always thought that his position was stronger than it was. He always pitched his terms too high.

In spite of Marston Moor he faced the end of the year with some confidence. In October another battle had been fought at Newbury, when three Roundhead armies had joined to destroy him.

They had failed, partly because of the king's own skill and partly because the Earl of Manchester was now deeply suspicious of Cromwell's growing power and did not want to beat the king altogether. He, too, wanted a peace.

Cromwell and Fairfax, however, wanted victory. They vainly urged that Charles should be pursued before he had joined Rupert. The other generals did not agree. After two years of war they saw that their armies were falling into ruin and mutiny.

Charles met Rupert and combined forces with him. The king was safe for another winter.

It was a winter of bitter argument in London. Two parties had formed at Westminster out of the hundred or so members who were left.

The stronger party favored the Scots. They wished to establish the Church on the Scottish Presbyterian pattern. They meant, if they could, to force everybody to belong to it. Their hopes were pinned on the strength of the Scottish army.

The other party was made up of men who thought as Cromwell did. They wanted freedom to worship as they pleased. They were beginning to think that they had fought for nothing.

There was one thing, however, that both parties agreed on. They hated bishops and Roman Catholics. Most of all, they hated Archbishop Laud, who had been in their power for a long while. So they brought him to trial.

Laud had been one of Charles's favorites in the days before the war. He was a little red-faced man with a quick temper and a high opinion of himself.

Acting as the king's chief servant in England, he had inflicted some savage punishments on those who resisted his tyranny.

In 1632, for instance, a man called Prynne had written a book against the theater. It was called *A Scourge of Stage Players*, and a scourge it certainly was.

Prynne said some very rude things in it about people who went to the theater. Laud decided that Prynne was hitting at King Charles and Queen Henrietta Maria, who were both fond of plays. So Archbishop Laud hauled the author before the Court of the Star Chamber.

This Star Chamber Court had been set up by other

kings many years before. Its real purpose was to punish great nobles who were too powerful for ordinary judges and juries to deal with. The culprit in the Star Chamber had little chance of a fair trial if the king was bent upon breaking him.

Laud accused poor Prynne of high treason. He was sentenced to be imprisoned for life, to pay a fine of £5,000, to lose his standing as a lawyer, to be set in the pillory and to have both his ears cropped.

The sentence was carried out; but even in jail Prynne went on writing his dangerous books. So, five years later, he was branded on both cheeks.

Another man, John Lilburne, twenty years old, was accused of printing Puritan books in Holland. He was flogged, set in the pillory and thrown into prison without food or money. Only the kindness of other prisoners kept him from starving to death.

These things were remembered against Archbishop Laud. He had done them because he had been trying to bring order into the Church. He and his partner, the Earl of Strafford, both prided themselves on being thorough.

They believed that people should do as the king ordered. In their eyes, men like Prynne and Lilburne were the worst kind of criminals, to be stamped on like so many poisonous snakes. It was small wonder that they had made themselves hated.

But because Strafford was so much cleverer than Laud he had been dealt with first. He was more dangerous, too dangerous to be left alive. Parliament had brought him to the executioner's block in May 1641.

That was before the war had started, while the king was still in London. Charles had been forced to sign his servant's death warrant from fear of the London mob, which had roamed the streets shouting for Strafford's execution and threatening the safety of the royal family.

But the king's signature was not necessary in 1645. The war had been raging for three years by then. In London, Laud's enemies could do what they wished. On January 10th the Archbishop was beheaded. Prynne and Lilburne were avenged.

The execution satisfied some of the fiercer rebels but it did nothing to win the war. The Roundhead armies were falling into mutiny. Deserters were everywhere. Men were refusing duty and even attacking their officers. Unpaid and disorderly, they roamed the country-side and terrorized the people.

Things were made worse by quarrels in Parliament. Cromwell was accusing the Earl of Manchester of causing the failure at the second battle of Newbury. Manchester declared that Cromwell was seeking to overthrow the nobility. The House of Lords backed Manchester and the House of Commons backed Cromwell.

The bad state of the armies, however, was frightening everybody. Something had to be done. Either they would have to make peace or create a new and different army.

First they tried to make peace. They sent messengers

93

to Charles, who answered them firmly, "There are three things I will not part with — the Church, my crown and my friends; and you will have much ado to get them from me."

In spite of this, the peace talks dragged on throughout the winter. But while some were talking, others were acting. When the talks broke down, in February 1645, the plans for the New Model Army were well under way.

Parliament had learned the lessons of the war at last. Cromwell's Ironsides had shown what kind of an army was needed. There must be an end to the old, unruly levies that had vexed both sides. The new army must be willing to march and fight anywhere.

Until 1645 most of the men had been recruited for local service. As soon as the fighting had gone beyond their county boundaries, they had packed off home to look after their neglected trades and families. This meant that neither king nor Parliament could drive a deathblow home. As soon as they advanced, their trained men began to melt away.

It was a wonder that the Cornishmen had marched with Hopton as far as Lansdown. It was a miracle that the Londoners had gone so far from home to relieve Gloucester. The Roundhead leaders now decided that such miracles must become everyday events.

They planned to raise 21,000 men and pay them regularly. Most of them would come from the armies of Waller, Essex and Manchester; the rest would be pressed into service. All would be dressed in the red coats which now, for the first time, became the English soldier's regular uniform.

The House of Lords did not like the idea of this new army. They guessed that its ranks would be filled with men whose heads were full of dangerous notions. There was too much talk of liberty and equality about.

Such men would need safe leaders, they decided. Colonel Cromwell must be kept out at all costs. But who could be chosen for command?

Essex, Waller and Manchester were all under a cloud. Their warlike fame did not compare with Cromwell's. It was difficult to pass Cromwell over, especially as he had many friends among his fellow members in the Commons.

It was these very friends who now seemed to give the Lords their chance. They passed a Self-Denying Ordinance which ruled that no member of either house should hold a command. This meant that Cromwell must choose between being a general and being an M.P. It would limit his growing power.

The Lords were pleased to agree to Sir Thomas Fairfax as Commander-in-Chief. Under him, old Philip Skippon would command the infantry. Both were safe men. Even if Cromwell decided to take command of the cavalry he would be unable to act alone.

This command of cavalry was therefore left open. Cromwell could have it if he resigned from Parliament, but not otherwise. His enemies felt satisfied that they had been very clever. They were all the more pleased because they had also had their way in another matter.

Parliament had now decided that the English Church should become Presbyterian like the Scottish one. The Independents hated the idea but did not oppose it too strongly. Above everything else they wanted to beat the king. They wanted to get on with the war.

The important thing was that the best colonels, majors and captains should be chosen to lead the new regiments. If a great many of them happened to be Independents, that was only the result of the war. Cromwell's Ironsides had fought better than anybody else.

So the recruiting began and the men came in, some as volunteers but nearly half as dejected conscripts. From the very beginning, however, the discipline was severe. Fines were imposed for swearing, floggings for disobedience and even harsher punishments for more serious offenses.

Drilling began on the fields of Windsor. It was conducted by men who knew what they were about, men who had proved themselves in countless skirmishes and in half-a-dozen battles.

One wishes one could have been there to hear some of their quaintly given orders.

"Now at the word *Order your Pikes* you place the butt end of your pike by the outside of your right foot, your right hand holding it even with your eye and your thumb right up; then your left arm being set akimbo by your side you shall stand with a full body in a comely posture."

While this kind of instruction was being given to the pikemen, the musketeers would also be learning their craft. There were dozens of orders they had to know and obey.

The mounted troopers, too, would be practicing with their horses. They would wheel and turn and come on at the brisk trot which Cromwell had taught his men. They would learn to respond instantly to the trumpet call, while the infantry answered to the drum.

One of the finest armies in history was being built at Windsor in those early months of 1645. The redcoats moved in shifting patterns across the wide fields. The days lengthened and the pace quickened. The New Model Army was to be ready in May.

But the drums and the trumpets and the orders spoke only to the body of the army. Its strong heart was the independent spirit of freeborn Englishmen.

In the alehouses and in the billets the men talked together of the things they were fighting for. They listened to others whose eloquence had been nurtured in marketplace and meetinghouse. The words of the Bible echoed in their ears until they saw themselves as a new Israel fighting the battles of the Lord.

For some there was a Promised Land ahead, a land where men would be not only free, but equal, too! These men were the Levelers, the growing party which the House of Lords had feared. They were brave, intelligent and outspoken.

"What were the Lords of England," asked one of them, "but William the Conqueror's colonels? What were the barons but his majors, and the knights but his captains?"

Such questions as these were bandied about between

the soldiers. They listened to the fiery preachers who had joined them. One of these, a parson called Hugh Peters, declared that there ought never to be a single beggar in England.

There were even wilder spirits who shocked the respectable by saying that if they met King Charles in battle they would kill him as willingly as they would kill anybody else. In the ranks of the New Model, the age-old respect for tradition and titles and property was dwindling fast.

But there was soon work for the soldiers to do. In April of 1645 the old generals began to lay down their commands. Essex, Waller and Manchester retired from the army, while the Earl of Warwick handed over his command of the navy. The Self-Denying Ordinance was in force.

Cromwell, it seemed, had decided that his place was in the House of Commons. He handed over his two fine cavalry regiments to his old comrade, Sir Thomas Fairfax, who accepted them gratefully as the senior regiment of the new army.

He added blue facings to their new scarlet uniforms and gave them the proud title of the General's Troop. Henceforth they would be one regiment instead of two. In the following June they rode with Fairfax to Newport Pagnell.

They must have been regretting that their old leader was no longer with them. Cromwell had returned not to Westminster but to his home in East Anglia. There among his friends and neighbors he was raising fresh troops from the Puritan towns and homesteads of that rich and level countryside.

It was no time for debate, but for action. King Charles was once more in the field, somewhere near Daventry. The New Model Army was marching north to meet him.

With battle threatening, General Fairfax called a council of war. The grim, red-coated colonels assembled to hear what he and Skippon had to say. There was swift agreement about what was needed.

A commander for the cavalry must be found and there was only one man good enough. Let Parliament say what it liked about the Self-Denying Ordinance. Oliver Cromwell must be Lieutenant General whether he was an M.P. or not.

Sir Thomas at once appointed his friend to the vacant command. He sent messages to Cromwell and to Parliament, telling them what he had done.

On June 13th, in the cold chill of early morning, Cromwell rode into camp at the head of six hundred men. There was a great storm of cheering to welcome him, but there was little time for much else.

The king had halted at Naseby, only a few miles away. Plans had to be made immediately. The next day, on June 14th, the two armies aligned themselves to face the last great battle of the Civil War.

VIII

Naseby

The early summer of 1645 had been rainy, and the fields around the village of Naseby were damp and spongy. The ditches were brimming brightly. The ground would obviously hinder the proper use of cavalry.

All this Fairfax realized in the early morning of June 14th. He began, therefore, to shift his position in search of a drier spot.

Prince Rupert, with his eyes on the foe, thought for

a while that the Roundheads were afraid to fight. He ordered his own army to move in an attempt to out-flank them.

For a long while this cautious sparring went on, un-til the two enemy hosts faced each other across the drier ground of Broadmoor, a mile or so north of Naseby village.

The Roundheads outnumbered the Royalists and were drawn up on a ridge overlooking Broadmoor. The king's forces were on another ridge to the north. Both sides felt confident about the outcome of the day.

As usual, the King's Foot was in the center. They were flanked, on the king's side, by Rupert's horse on their right and by Sir Marmaduke Langdale's on their left. Facing Rupert, this time, was not Cromwell but Henry Ireton, a young and able soldier who was later to marry Cromwell's daughter.

In support of Ireton was Colonel Okey. He had thronged a nearby hedge with a thousand dragoons. This hedge stretched from the Roundhead lines toward the enemy, so that when Rupert attacked he would have to run the gauntlet of Okey's fire.

Cromwell was on the other wing, facing Sir Marm-aduke Langdale across some very rough ground, crowded with furze bushes and honeycombed with rabbit holes.

Between Cromwell's cavalry and Ireton's stood the well-drilled infantry of the New Model, still lacking in experience but looking very splendid in their bright red coats. Old Philip Skippon was commanding them and wondering how they would behave when the battle started.

It began with Rupert's charge. His reckless cavaliers pressed forward past the length of Okey's hedge. The dragoons poured in fire from their leafy shelter but the attackers swept onward. They reached the foot of the ridge and set their horses at the slope.

Ireton ordered his men forward to meet them. The Roundhead cavalry came over the brow of the hill, which until then had been hiding their numbers. For the first time, Rupert saw the size of Ireton's force.

He halted, apparently in surprise. The cautious Ireton failed to press home his advantage. He halted too, and began to dress his ranks. Before he had finished doing it Rupert charged home.

Some of Ireton's men charged to meet him, but the rest hung back. Within a few minutes Rupert's men were once again chasing a beaten enemy.

In the center, the king's trusty infantry was coming to grips with Skippon's. Using their pikes and muskets vigorously, the Royalists soon broke some of the new regiments; but the enemy's reserves stood firm under Sir Thomas Fairfax.

Meanwhile Ireton, who had not fled with the rest of his men, had managed to collect a party of his scattered horse. He looked around for something he could do. Seeing the danger of Skippon's position, he rode with his men to the rescue.

But the king's men had been charged before by

stronger forces than Ireton's. They swept his riders aside, wounded Ireton himself and took him prisoner. Things were looking black for Parliament.

A charge now by Rupert could have ended the day in a royal victory. But the prince, hard though it is to believe, had still not learned the lessons of Edgehill and Marston Moor. He was away at his old game of plundering the Parliamentary wagons.

After galloping a mile he reached his prey, only to find that the New Model had provided for his arrival. A special company of sharpshooters had been formed to protect the supplies. They met the Cavaliers with a brisk volley which sent them riding back to the battle-field.

Meanwhile even Cromwell was in some difficulty. Because of the bad ground he had been unable to advance his men in unbroken formation. The spiky barrier of gorse and the crumbling ground of the rabbit warren had broken the force of his charge.

Hard fighting now failed to rout Langdale's men. The most the Ironsides could do was to force the enemy back to a rallying point behind the king's army. There Langdale halted, ready to rejoin the fray as soon as the chance came.

Cromwell did not mean to give him such a chance. He sent some of his regiments to watch Langdale and then eyed the rest of the battle to see where he could do most good.

The fighting in the center was still raging, but there

were plenty of men busy there already. Cromwell decided to attack the king's reserve, which had so far not been engaged.

With three regiments he charged down upon it, but without immediate success. The King's Foot resisted with their usual stubborn valor. There was no sign that they would either retreat or break. Cromwell fought on, wondering no doubt how soon it would be before Prince Rupert returned.

Then, at the critical moment, somebody in the Royalist army made a dread blunder. A voice was raised high in an order to the infantry.

"To the right! Turn! March!"

The whole of Charles's reserve obeyed, sweeping the king with it to join Langdale's cavalry in the rear. Soon Rupert joined them with his winded and useless horses. It was too late to do anything except watch.

It was left to the king's humble infantry to bear the cost of the day. Still fighting boldly, they must have thought that victory was theirs. They did not at first know that they were alone.

But they quickly learned. While their plumed and mounted comrades watched from a distance, the foot were hemmed in by the whole Roundhead army.

Colonel Okey called out his dragoons from their sheltering hedge and ordered them to mount. With blazing flintlocks they bore down on the enemy's left. Meanwhile, Cromwell's Ironsides were pistoling and hacking their way in from the right.

The helpless royal infantry could make no headway

against the weight of Skippon's men in front. Their retreat was cut off by Ireton's rallied troopers, who were harrying their rear.

It was surrender or die, but many even then refused to throw down their arms. One whole brigade, distinguished by their blue coats and by their valor, fought to the last man. When the sun went down on the bloodstained litter of Naseby Field the king's infantry had ceased to exist.

By then, however, Charles was miles away. Perhaps he was already planning to fight again another day. He had lost battles before, and had found fresh armies when he needed them. Most of his precious cavalry was safe, and he had other forces in the south and west. There were grounds for hope.

But for Charles there were to be no more big battles. This time he had lost more than a few thousand brave foot soldiers. This time he had lost the war.

The weary victors turned to count the spoil. From the trampled grass they picked up the limp standards of the defeated. They collected pikes and muskets by the thousands and wagons by the dozens.

Charles had lost all his guns and all his ammunition. Most dangerous of all, his private letters had been captured. In them his enemies could read the full story of his double-dealing.

Given time, he could have repaired all this. There were thousands of men in the hills of Wales who would follow him gladly. There was a chance that help might come from Ireland. There was even some hope in Scotland.

The defeat of Naseby would not have mattered if it had happened in 1644. Now, however, there was a new power in England, a force that could follow wherever he went and defeat him wherever he stood. The New Model Army had mastered the kingdom.

As yet, however, it did not know its strength. It had won a single battle and might easily have lost it. Many of its men were still newcomers to the soldier's deadly trade. They needed practice.

So Charles was not pursued in the days that followed Naseby. He reached Hereford and halted in its hilly borderland. He began again to recruit his loyal Welshmen. The Scottish army moved south to keep an eye on him.

The New Model marched away into Dorset and found itself confronted by hundreds of Clubmen, roaming a countryside which was desperate for peace. Fairfax, who knew when to be kind, settled the trouble without bloodshed. His army was well supplied. He did not need to rob the villagers of their bread. The Clubmen dispersed to their homes.

Then Fairfax settled down to mop up the Royalist garrisons one by one. Their resistance was sometimes sharp but never powerful. The Royalists were losing support as they became harsher in their dealings with the people.

They were in a corner and they knew it. For them, it was now all or nothing.

"Rest not upon the curiosity of quaint distinctions," wrote Lord Culpeper to Lord Digby from Barnstaple in Devon. "A kingdom is at stake!"

Culpeper was afraid that Digby was sticking too closely to the rules, but there were others who had forgotten all about them. Another Royalist records, "We had in our company soldiers so unruly that gave the whole county an alarm against us; they would ride out on every hand and rob the carriages."

Such men as these were throwing the king's last hopes to the winds. Compared with the disciplined soldiers of the New Model they were little better than highwaymen and brigands. The country would not support them.

In vain, the better sort tried to keep up resistance. The royal strongholds yielded one after the other. Where they did not, General Fairfax crushed them with his growing weight of cannon.

While he was clearing the southwest the tide of war had also turned in Wales. Roundhead forces overran Pembroke and moved north, nudging Charles out of Hereford and away into Yorkshire. Finding no comfort there, the unhappy king wandered back toward Huntingdon.

It was there at last that good news reached him from Scotland. The Marquis of Montrose had raised a Royalist revolt in the Highlands. Leading his wild clansmen on swift marches across their native mountains, he had surprised and defeated one force after another.

Then he had marched toward the Lowlands. At Kil-

MARQUIS OF MONTROSE

syth near Glasgow he had won a great victory. In all Scotland there was no army to oppose him.

It seemed that if Charles had lost one kingdom the brave Montrose had now gained him another. The king sent messages urging Montrose to come to his aid. He himself prepared to move north to join the marquis.

There was dire news, however, from elsewhere. Prince Rupert had been cornered in Bristol by General Fairfax. A brief cannonade had convinced him of the power of the enemy's artillery. To save the lives of his men he tamely surrendered the city.

Charles could not believe it. Such behavior was the last thing to be expected of his rash and adventurous nephew. When Rupert came riding in to explain, the angry king would not listen.

There was a fine quarrel between them which ended with Rupert being dismissed. He stalked out of the royal presence and began to make plans for leaving England.

Meanwhile, the letters Charles had lost at Naseby were being read and published by his enemies in London. They showed that he had never intended to make peace. They proved that he was not to be trusted an inch.

There were others letters also which were being read in London. They came from Cromwell and they reported a growing number of victories. The mopping up of the Royalists was going well.

Cromwell, however, kept reminding Parliament who was winning the battles.

"Honest men served you faithfully in this action," he wrote about one victory. "They are trusty. Do not discourage them."

Again he wrote, "In things of the mind we look for no compulsion as far as conscience will admit."

Quietly and sensibly he was trying to warn the men in London not to drive the soldiers too far. He knew that the pro-Scottish party was planning to force the army to become Presbyterian. He realized the trouble that would bring.

At first there was little danger. Montrose was winning in Scotland and this meant that the Scots in England were kept busy. Presently, however, there was other news.

Montrose had come a little too far south for safety. His Highlanders, laden with plunder, were beginning to feel the call of the distant glens. They began to melt away into the misty north.

With dwindled numbers, the marquis suddenly found himself trapped. His small force was defeated and he had to flee for his life. With him went the king's greatest hope.

The Presbyterians in London smiled and rubbed their hands. The news was good everywhere. Even Prince Rupert was in favor of peace. He sent to Westminster and asked for safe-conduct to leave the country. With a band of faithful friends he sailed away.

The Scottish army in England was now free to act. It could help to fasten the Scottish religion on to an unwilling England. First, however, the New Model Army must be put out of the way.

That could be done as soon as Charles surrendered. His cause was now falling into ruin everywhere. The queen was already safely in France, busying her pen with pages of advice to her cornered husband. Some of her letters were captured also. They did Charles more harm than ever.

There were some Royalists, however, who were still

fighting bravely for their king. The gallant Hopton, pushed farther and farther west, tried to defend the Devonshire town of Torrington against Fairfax.

Again he was the victim of an accident. Fifty barrels of gunpowder exploded in the church and scattered fragments of timber and masonry all over the town. There was nothing Hopton could do except retreat. He and the survivors limped back into Cornwall.

On March 16, 1646, he surrendered. Of all the Royalist leaders he had the most reason to be proud. Neither he nor his men had ever faltered.

It was the end in the southwest. The Prince of Wales, now aged sixteen, took ship for the Isles of Scilly. In little groups the Royalists gave themselves up or sailed from the land they loved.

By strange chance it was old Sir Jacob Astley who fought the last fight. Sir Jacob had a gift for saying memorable things. It was his prayer, uttered at Edgehill, which began this book.

On March 21, 1646, he brought the king's last little army to Stow-on-the-Wold, a lonely town set in the steep Cotswold Hills. Sir Jacob had three thousand men to face the day.

Three Roundhead commanders combined their forces and smashed Sir Jacob's regiments. It was soon over, that final battle, but it is still remembered in Stow-on-the-Wold. There is today an interesting little museum there which is full of Civil War relics.

But Sir Jacob's memory may outlast the steel with which he fought. After the battle he squatted comfortably on a drum and gazed around mockingly at his captors.

His white head nodded wisely as he spoke the words that ended the First Civil War.

"You have now done your work and may go play ... unless you fall out among yourselves."

IX

The Agitators

The year 1646 was one of disorder and strange homecomings. Back to the villages and manor houses came the defeated Royalists. Their pockets were empty and their hearts were full.

Those lonely riders, jogging home, were men who had promised never to fight again. The others, who would not promise, were rotting in prisons or beginning desperate, threadbare lives in the taverns and gaming houses of foreign cities.

113

For the man who came home there was much to do. He had a heavy fine to pay for his loyalty. It might be a fifth or even a half of all he possessed. While he pinched and scraped to raise the money he saw his late enemies being rewarded from the public purse.

There were gutted homes to be rebuilt, fences, barns and cottages to repair, herds and flocks to be replenished. For the poor man there was work to find in a land where bread was twice as dear as it had been before.

There were new taxes to meet on soap, salt, paper, cloth and many other things. A laborer's wages had gone up from sevenpence to eightpence a day, but the extra penny did little to cover all these rising costs.

No wonder that men began to scowl at the red-coated troopers who rode around the countryside for two whole shillings a day. It was time, murmured many, to disband the army now that the war was over.

The growing discontent gave King Charles some grounds for hope. His enemies were an ill-assorted band. If he could make them quarrel with each other, he might yet return to London in triumph.

He began by writing letters to Fairfax and Cromwell. His plan was to set them against Parliament, but they saw the trap and did not reply. Charles then turned his attention to the Scottish generals.

With them he had better luck. In May 1646 he rode into the Scottish camp and gave himself up. He was given all the honor due to his exalted rank, and began to pride himself on his own cleverness. Surrounded by the armed men of his northern kingdom, he felt safe to pursue his tricky policy.

But the Scots were stubborn in their demands. Time and again they came back to two conditions. Charles must get rid of his bishops and he must give up his royal right to the armed forces.

Charles meant to do neither. As he saw it, neither the Church nor the rights of the Crown were his to surrender. He had received them from God in trust for those who came after him. It was a trust that he would not betray.

But he did not shrink from double-dealing. "Keep the militia!" urged Queen Henrietta Maria in her letters to him. That brave and silly woman was already plotting a new war. She was busying herself in Europe, trying to raise Roman Catholic troops to rescue her husband.

Charles wrote back to assure her that he was "playing his game." In that game he was making up the rules as he went along. In his mind, the men who had beaten him were rogues and rebels who deserved nothing better than to be tricked and hanged.

They were, however, better players than he was. The Scots presently realized that keeping him was a poor bargain. They made a better one with the English Parliament. For a large sum of money they handed over the king and agreed to march their army back home.

Charles was sent south, to Holmby House, near Northampton. "I am bought and sold," he declared bitterly. He had taken a long step toward his doom, but he did not realize it. His hopes were raised again by the quarrel which was beginning between Parliament and the English soldiers.

The promises that had been made to the men of the New Model Army were being broken. The troops were becoming anxious about the future. They began to listen to men like Edward Sexby of Suffolk, an intelligent and forceful trooper of Cromwell's old regiment.

Sexby had joined Cromwell in 1643. Now, in 1646, he was still a private soldier in the new regiment that had been formed under Sir Thomas Fairfax.

Like his comrades, he had become a soldier to fight for freedom. He now realized that his freedom was in greater danger than ever.

Sexby pointed out to his comrades what was happening. He, and others like him in every regiment, began to list their grievances.

They did not intend to be forced in matters of religion. They were not willing to become Presbyterians just because Parliament ordered it.

This was their main grievance, but there were others as well. Sexby and all his friends were growing angry about the absence of pay. The promises made to them had not been kept, and their pockets were emptier every day.

Worse still, perhaps, and the height of unfairness, was that soldiers were being hauled before the magistrates and punished for things they had done in the service of Parliament. A stolen bundle of hay, long forgotten, might now be brought against some luckless trooper, who found himself being tried at the assizes before an unsympathetic judge.

For a long while, however, the men were patient. They had arms in their hands and felt that as long as they stuck together something would have to be done for them. It was not until Parliament moved against them that they decided to act.

The men in London were bent upon getting rid of the dangerous force they had created. They decided to disband some regiments and send the rest to Ireland. They probably thought they were dealing with simple, ignorant fellows, but they had not reckoned on men like Sexby.

The troops met together and made a protest to Fairfax. Before they went to Ireland, they said, they wanted their back pay and they wanted to know who their generals in Ireland would be.

Fairfax heard them out and then went to London and did his best for them. When he returned he brought bad news. Parliament would pay only six weeks of the back money due to the soldiers, and had made Skippon and Massey the generals for the Irish war.

The answer was plain enough for Sexby. Six weeks' pay was only a small part of what was owing. Generals Skippon and Massey were both Presbyterians. Sexby and his friends knew that they must act at once.

117

Something now happened which was quite new in England. The rank and file met together and chose their own leaders, two from each regiment. They gave them the name of Agitators and made them agents for the common soldier.

These Agitators wrote to their generals and claimed that Parliament was trying to ruin the army and break it to pieces. Parliament grew alarmed and sent Cromwell and his friends to soothe the angry troops.

They met at Saffron Walden, a quiet little town on the borders of Essex. A lot of promises were made and the men quieted down. But they did not change their minds.

By that time Edward Sexby had had a rare experience, the first of many like it in his eventful life. He had ridden with two of his comrades, Allen and Sheppard, right into London Town and had faced an angry Parliament.

Firmly they made their demands. They were sure of the justice of their cause and they were certain of the backing of twenty thousand armed men. Their bearing gave Parliament an unpleasant surprise. The army was even more dangerous than it had feared.

The men in London now tried something else. They ordered the regiments to march to widely separated places. Thus, they hoped, they could disband the men without trouble.

All this time Cromwell must have been slowly making up his mind what to do. It was always his way to seek God's guidance in every step he took. His enemies mocked him for this, and some do so even now.

They pointed out that God usually seemed to decide on whatever was best for Oliver Cromwell, but to argue like this is hardly being fair.

Cromwell was living at a time when law and justice had been overthrown. It was not his fault that there were many different parties all trying to outwit each other. When his enemies were scheming and worrying, Oliver Cromwell would often be praying.

While he was on his knees his enemies frequently made a mistake. It was natural enough for Cromwell to decide then that God had made His plans clear. Once that had been done Cromwell would carry out those plans to the end.

So it was now. He saw that he could not desert the army. If he and his officers did not lead it, there were men like Edward Sexby who could and would.

Cromwell acted swiftly. He persuaded Fairfax to order the whole army to meet at Newmarket. It was their first open disobedience to Parliament, but Cromwell followed it with something else.

He called a meeting of officers at his house in London. They were careful not to tell Fairfax what they decided there. A cavalry officer, Cornet Joyce, was ordered to ride for Northampton and pick up five hundred horsemen on his way.

He arrived at Holmby House where the king was staying and was ushered into the royal presence. For his own safety the king must go elsewhere, urged Joyce respectfully. The king came out of the house and stood looking at the steady lines of helmeted troopers waiting in front of it.

"Where is your commission?" he asked Joyce.

The officer was nonplussed for a moment. Then he jerked his thumb over his shoulder toward his men.

"There it is," he said.

The king's pale face bore a smile when he answered.

"It is as fair a commission and as well written as any I have seen in my life," he declared. When Joyce offered to let him choose where he would like to go, the king decided on Newmarket.

Meanwhile, the innocent Fairfax had played his part in the plot. Horse, foot and gun, the army marshaled itself on Triploe Heath, near Cambridge. There was consternation in London. To the army's might, Cromwell had now added the king's right. Army and king together could do anything.

Parliament sent messengers speeding to talk with the soldiers, but it was now too late. The army knew its power. The troops listened coldly to what the envoys said. Then they turned to obey their generals.

By slow stages the long columns of redcoats bore down upon London. Parliament ordered Fairfax to withdraw, but it was now almost impossible for him to obey. Real revolutionaries were having their say as to what should be done. An Army Council had been formed.

Men like Edward Sexby and Colonel Rainborough were pressing toward a fight with Parliament. The

Army Council accused eleven M.P.s of plotting a new war and demanded that they should be turned out of Westminster. It demanded, too, that a new Parliament should be called. It asked to be shown accounts of what was happening to the country's money.

Meanwhile, the king was overjoyed at the way things were turning out. It was just what he had hoped for. The army was treating him very well, and he was certain that his own cleverness was reaping its reward.

But there were other men cleverer than he. They knew just what he was thinking.

"Sir," said keen-brained Henry Ireton, "you mean to be an arbitrator between Parliament and us. We mean to be the arbitrators between Your Majesty and Parliament."

The Army Council now tried to make peace by offering Charles the best possible terms. In an evil moment he decided not to accept them. He had heard rumors of trouble in London and thought he could do better by waiting.

The rumors were true enough. The citizens were trying their old game of rioting. It was a game that had gone well enough in the past, when John Pym had played it against King Charles.

The streets filled with shouting people, the closed and shuttered shops, the broken heads and looted houses had all seemed very frightening five years before; but the soldiers had seen worse things than that at Naseby and elsewhere. The London mob did not frighten the army.

121

It did, however, give the generals the very excuse they were looking for. They decided that Parliament must be protected against the angry citizens. When some fifty friendly M.P.s came and asked Fairfax for help, the troops went into action.

Fairfax rushed forces to seize the fort at Tilbury on the north bank of the Thames. He sent more men to Gravesend on the opposite side of the river. Between them, they cut the port of London off from the sea. It was exactly what Charles had hoped to do in 1643.

The rest of the army mustered its terrible strength on Hounslow Heath. Twenty thousand veterans made ready to move against the capital. The citizens made frantic preparations to resist.

At the south end of London Bridge, however, there was a weak spot. The people of Southwark, jealous of their neighbors, saw no reason why they should be butchered in London's quarrel. They went to Fairfax and asked him to help them.

At about two o'clock in the morning of August 4, 1647, the dark streets of Southwark echoed to the sound of thousands of horsemen. Four regiments had arrived under the command of the determined Colonel Rainborough.

Although the first rays of dawn had not yet begun to brighten the waters of the river, Rainborough knew exactly what to do. In pitch darkness his men set to work.

A witness tells us that, "finding the gates shut, and a portcullis let down at the bridge, and a guard within, they planted two pieces of ordnance at the gate, and set a guard without."

Those two silent guns were eloquent messengers. The fort yielded. In the early morning the rebel cavalry thundered across the bridge and entered the city.

There was now a deal of face-saving and hand-washing. It seemed that everybody had really been good friends all along. On August 5th in Hyde Park,

the lord mayor and aldermen met the general to congratulate the fair composure between the army and the city; and after some ceremony they marched toward Westminster in this order.

First, Colonel Hammond's regiment of foot, then Colonel Rich and Cromwell's regiment of horse, then the general on horseback with his lifeguard, then the Speaker and the Lords and Commons in coaches, and Tomlinson's regiment of horse brought up the rearguard. The general was accompanied by many officers and gentlemen that rode with him, and every soldier had a branch of laurel in his hat.

Almost everybody was there that day except King Charles. Yet the puzzle was how to govern the country either with him or without him. The army had the armed power, but only the king had the true lawful authority.

While Parliament tried to find some way out of its muddle it spared the time to do one or two things it thought necessary. On August 11th it ordered that

123

there should be no more stage plays, bullbaiting or "dancing on the ropes." London should be a gloomy place henceforth. Perhaps that would teach its mutinous citizens a lesson.

Apart from that Parliament did little. All seemed calm again. The king was brought to Hampton Court, where he began to waste everybody's time and patience in fresh discussions.

The Lord Mayor and Aldermen who had greeted Fairfax with such friendliness in Hyde Park were now clapped into jail for their share in the late rioting. Some M.P.s, who were just as guilty, left London hastily.

The Independents, Cromwell's friends, now had a clear majority in the Commons. There was in fact little of the House left. On October 9th, when Parliament met, there were one hundred and fifty members absent. They were fined twenty pounds each for being away.

The written records for the same day give us an amusing sidelight on what kind of men were now ruling England. They tell us: "The general council of the army had conference with a German, who gave himself out to be a prophet; and they considered of their own pay and the pay of the northern forces."

It was thus in everything they did. There was the same strange mixture of religion and worldly wisdom. But they were not hypocrites. To them, the affairs of this world and the next were mixed together. They believed fervently in what they were doing and they had risked their lives for it.

Some of them were ready to risk their lives again.

There was the growing party in the army, called Levelers, who wanted to divide up large estates and make an end of the nobility altogether. They saw no reason for keeping a king at all. They openly declared themselves in favor of a republic.

Cromwell was afraid of these extreme revolutionaries. To keep them in check he worked hard to make an agreement between the sensible men. Charles and the Presbyterians, however, could not see the dangers ahead. They went on with their plots.

They were both now counting on a Scottish invasion to turn the tables on the army. Plans were being laid to start a fresh war.

In November, Charles slipped away from Hampton Court and rode hard from London. As soon as he could he took refuge in the Isle of Wight. There, no doubt, he felt safer. It would be easy to escape from the island by sea, and he wanted to be out of the way of what he knew was coming.

As soon as his escape was known, the Levelers turned on Cromwell. They blamed him for letting the king go. Colonel Rainborough was especially threatening. He suspected Cromwell of playing a double game.

For the time being, Cromwell's position was dangerous. But again Fairfax stood by his friend. Between them they managed to keep the army in hand, but it was touch-and-go.

Open mutiny broke out on November 15th in two regiments at Ware. Cromwell lost his temper and drew his sword. He rode into the mutineers, striking out right and left. The terrified soldiers gave in, and delivered up one of the ringleaders to be shot.

All this was pleasant news for Charles, who was still playing his game from the fancied safety of the Isle of Wight. Some more captured letters showed Parliament that it was a waste of time talking with him. Cromwell and Ireton agreed.

They were working closely together with Fairfax. They knew that the Royalists were planning a new war and they knew that they were helpless to prevent it. How and where would it begin?

The army was unpopular, Parliament was only a name, and the king was growing in the people's favor every day. It was only a matter of time before somebody set a match to the powder barrel.

The man who did it was a certain Colonel Poyer, who seems to have been a little England in himself. He was as divided and as changeable as the whole realm.

Letters of complaint came from Pembroke to London. They said that Colonel Poyer had refused to give up a castle when ordered to do so. The letters reflect the writer's bewilderment at Poyer's behavior.

In the morning, Poyer is sober and penitent and in the afternoon he is drunk and full of plots. He put four or five of his companions into the best apparel he could get and, by sunrising, put them out at the sally-port, and received them in at the gate himself with great ceremony, giving out in the town that they

126

were commanders sent out of France to him from the Prince of Wales.

When he hears news that pleases him, he puts forth bloody colors and declares for King and Common Prayer; when he hears other news he is for the oath and covenant and puts forth blue-and-white colors. The one day he fired all his guns on Parliament's forces without any occasion, but afterwards was very quiet. Yet the next day he vowed that not one of Parliament's forces shall go away alive, and calls the general *King Thomas*.

It is clear enough to us that Colonel Poyer must have been an awkward man to deal with. He seems even to have been a little mad. If so, the madness was catching, for it was Poyer who started the Second Civil War.

X

The Game Ends

However long a storm may have been gathering, the first flash of lightning always brings surprise.

A body of disgruntled troops suddenly joined Colonel Poyer. This increase of strength was more than the colonel's mental balance could stand. He attacked the Parliamentary forces, routed them, and killed their commander. The whole of South Wales rose for the king.

It was too soon for the Royalist leaders. They had been waiting for the Scottish army to cross the border. When that happened, Cromwell and Fairfax would have to march north. They had planned their rebellion for that moment, but Poyer forced them to act at once, before the Scots were ready.

In Kent the people massed in their thousands and began to march on London. Part of the navy, which had been always loyal to Parliament, now changed sides. The sails of hostile warships were seen in the Thames. Detachments of sailors seized the castles at Deal, Walmer and Sandown.

Cromwell and Fairfax consulted each other anxiously. They decided to split their forces. Cromwell hurried west to deal with Poyer, while Fairfax moved to crush the rebels nearer home.

Eight thousand men marched into Kent and lay in the fields around Eltham all night. Next day they were on their way east in the direction of Dartford. The speed of their advance sent the enemy helter-skelter back to Maidstone.

Before they could organize their defenses Fairfax stormed the town and fought a bitter battle through its streets. Three thousand rebels fled to Rochester.

It was now neck or nothing for the Royalists. The army was in a revengeful mood and was using its strength ruthlessly. In South Wales, Cromwell was clearing the open country and driving the rebels back into strongholds.

Although it was by now early summer, the Scots had

not invaded the north. The Royalists hoped to hold out until those foreigners arrived. The three thousand men who had reached Rochester from Maidstone crossed the Medway and dodged back toward London. They were trusting that its discontented citizens would rise to help them.

The Londoners, however, had already seen the New Model at close quarters. They kept quiet. The Kentish rebels, not knowing which way to turn, crossed the Thames and entered Essex.

Fairfax followed by a shorter route. On the south bank of the Thames he collected a fleet of small boats and ferried his men across to Tilbury. Their horses, swimming alongside, darkened the bright waters with their lifted heads.

On the Essex shore the men formed up and set out for Chelmsford and Colchester. The fleeing Royalists banged shut the gates of Colchester just in time. The fastening was held only by an officer's cane during the first furious minutes of the Roundhead assault.

Fighting for all they held dear, the rebels flung back Fairfax from the burning suburbs and settled down to a siege. Sir Thomas counted his losses and sent for more artillery.

He knew that the rebels' only hope lay in the Scottish army, which was at last on the move. It crossed the border on July 8, 1648, and began looking for assistance from the English of the north. By August it had come no farther than Hornby in Lancashire.

During that miserable rainy summer the Royalists

in Colchester held out against growing hunger and a massive bombardment from Fairfax's cannon. They were pinning him down and keeping him from marching north to help Cromwell. They were praying for Cromwell's defeat.

He had now taken the last of the Welsh strongholds and was groping his way toward the Scots. No doubt he was feeling a grim relish at the prospect of coming to grips with his former allies.

On August 17th he fell upon the English Royalists just outside Preston and drove them back into the town. The battle raged across the river bridges, which were being held by Scottish soldiers.

Cromwell's veterans stormed toward the crossings, fought their way to the other side and broke through the Scottish army. But this was only a beginning. They had cut off the enemy foot from their supporting cavalry and now began to harry their retreat.

At Warrington they hammered the invaders again. Within a fortnight the Scottish army was destroyed. The hundreds of prisoners were herded together and asked whether they had been volunteers or pressed men.

Cromwell now showed that the New Model was in an ugly mood. This time there was no forgiveness for the enemy. The volunteers were shipped off to the West Indies to labor like slaves in the sugar plantations. Only the pressed men were allowed to begin their perilous journey home through a hostile land.

At Colchester, which surrendered on August 27th,

Fairfax was also severe. Two of the leaders, Lucas and Lyle, were shot out of hand. Both died bravely.

Lucas tore open his doublet as he faced the firing squad. With his breast bared he told the soldiers not to miss. Grimly the musketeers assured him that they would not miss at that range.

"I have been closer than that when you have missed me," Lucas mocked them.

The boom of their muskets sounded the king's death knell. The shooting of brave men who had fought fairly was something new. If lesser culprits could pay with their lives for the havoc they had made, why should Charles Stuart escape unscathed?

This was the reasoning of the simple soldiers. The king was the real cause of the war. He had brought a foreign army to invade England. If that was not treason, then what was?

The army leaders had even more reason for bitterness. While the revolt was going on, the Presbyterians in Parliament had seized their chance. They had begun talks again with Charles.

It must have seemed to the generals that the country was a mad merry-go-round of plot and counterplot, with the king at the center, keeping the whole thing turning. There could be no peace while he lived.

Henry Ireton went even further than this. He argued that both Charles and his sons should be tried and condemned. But Fairfax shrank from this proposal. He made a last attempt to bring Charles to see reason.

When this failed, Cromwell at last decided that God's will was made plain.

As usual, what other men dared to say, Oliver Cromwell dared to do. On December 2, 1648, after taking the king from Carisbrooke Castle in the Isle of Wight, the troops entered London again.

Four days later, Colonel Pride marched a detachment of soldiers to Westminster. He halted them outside the House of Commons early in the morning and then waited for the members to arrive.

As they came they were closely watched by the colonel. He had a man standing by his side and pointing out which were the army's enemies. These were curtly told by Pride to go home again.

Those who resisted were at once arrested. They were packed off to a nearby house which rejoiced in the name of Hell Tavern, and were kept there all night in fear and discomfort. All this was done without Fairfax's approval, but Oliver Cromwell openly agreed with it.

"Black Tom" Fairfax, popular though he was with the troops, was now helpless. The safe general, whom Parliament had made commander of the New Model Army, was brushed aside by the revolutionaries. Their word was now the only law.

The rest of their work had to be done inside Parliament. It naturally fell to Oliver Cromwell, who was still a member of the Commons. After the purge by Colonel Pride he had little opposition.

One hundred and fifty members had been persuaded

133

by Pride that Westminster was an unhealthy place for them. When Cromwell took his seat he was thanked by the House for his victories in the north.

The tiny Parliament that was left soon gained a nickname. The "Rump," as it was called, was Cromwell's to do as he liked with. But in the dire task ahead Cromwell knew he would be almost alone, treading a path as narrow and dangerous as the edge of his sword. One slip would cost him everything.

We can never know all that was in his troubled mind. There are still people, and there were more then, who see him only as a man seeking power for himself. But this is hard to believe when we remember how slowly he reached it.

Three long years had gone by since the victories of Naseby. During all that time, there had never been a day when Charles could not have made a lasting peace. It was not Cromwell's fault that he did not.

It was not truly Charles's fault, either. These were two men who, both in their own way, wanted peace and honor for England. The king knew that on him alone depended the future of the Crown. Cromwell knew that on him alone depended freedom.

In the clash between them, they both risked everything. By January 1649 it was really Charles who had the easier part to play.

He was no coward, but he had been stupid and vain and willful. He had tried tyranny, he had tried armed force and he had tried cunning. All had failed him.

134

Now he had only his faith and courage left.

His enemies began to strip from his life all the courtly ceremony that had once surrounded him. Perhaps they were trying to show the people of England, watching with anxious eyes, that here was only a wicked man, fit for the gallows.

If so, they failed. In the bareness of this altered life, with the false glitter of the court denied him, the king showed himself more clearly than ever before.

His small, slight figure, his dark clothes and melancholy eyes needed no herald. When he faced his judges in the winter gloom of Westminster Hall, they knew, and all England knew, that Charles was king indeed.

There had been some trouble in collecting those judges together. In what they had to do, Cromwell and his friends wanted as many accomplices as possible. Altogether they had chosen one hundred and thirty-five men.

Of these only fifty-two presented themselves. Fairfax came once but never again. When his name was called, his wife answered for him from the gallery:

"He has more wit than to be here!"

Other men copied his example. Out of those who remained, a lawyer called Bradshaw allowed himself to be raised to the perilous post of President of the Court. The trial was fixed for January 20, 1649.

A lot of work had gone into making Westminster Hall fit for the occasion. Benches had been put up for the judges. Galleries had been erected for important spectators.

The king was surrounded by red-coated soldiers under the command of Colonel Hacker. More troops under Colonel Axtell were lining the walls and guarding the doors. They stood watchfully, ready to move at once if there were any interference by the People of England.

Charles looked carefully around the courtroom and then sat down without removing his hat. He was determined to show from the beginning that this was no lawful trial. Justice came from God and the king, not from armed force. He would not show respect for such an assembly as this.

Cromwell and Ireton were watching, but only a few other important officers were present. Through the courtroom came the sound of Bradshaw's north-country voice. The trial had begun.

The king tried to interrupt the lengthy accusation which was read out, but Bradshaw would not let him speak. When the charge was ended the king laughed. Bradshaw now challenged him to answer.

The king replied quickly. He demanded to know on what lawful power the court rested. Until he knew that, declared Charles, he would plead neither guilty nor not guilty. If they had the right to try him, let them prove it before they began.

A long wrangle followed. The king had the better of the argument and even gained some applause from the bolder spectators who were ready to risk Cromwell's frowns. At last Bradshaw brought the day's work to an end. Nothing had been done, but they would try again on Monday.

Monday went no better, although there was more excitement. There was a good deal of shouting from people inside and outside the court. The soldiers restored order, but it was plain to Cromwell that the king was winning more sympathy every day.

On Tuesday evening they had got no further. The number of judges had dwindled. By the time Thursday came there were only thirty-one of them left on the benches.

It was on Friday that Cromwell came at last to a dreadful decision. If the king continued not to plead, he must be sentenced without trial. Before Saturday dawned the death warrant was ready.

It was on this day that Lady Fairfax made another bold interruption from the public gallery. Colonel Axtell ordered his soldiers to present their muskets and fire if she spoke another word. The threat worked. The court continued its sorry task.

Then came a more dangerous upset. One of the judges, Colonel Downes, rallied his sinking courage and rose from his seat. Cromwell tried to bully him into silence but Downes managed to voice a protest.

With the judges quarreling among themselves, Bradshaw had to order the court to retire. Downes was then invited to explain his interruption. Cromwell spoke to him roughly.

He called Downes peevish and ordered Bradshaw

back into court to do his duty. Colonel Downes trem-blingly faced his general's awful wrath. He said there were others there who had the same opinions as him-self.

"Call them! Call them!" shouted Cromwell, who seemed to be in a state bordering on madness.

Downes spoke some names, but the cravens did not budge to help him. Cromwell turned on the luckless colonel even more dangerously than before. He accused him of trying to make a mutiny in the army. It was a plain threat that he might be shot.

Another man, who was perhaps trying to shield the colonel, suggested that Downes was off his head. Amid jeering laughter Colonel Downes slunk away, leaving his name to history as that of a truly brave man.

There were no more protests. The rest of them bun-dled back into court. On that day they sentenced the king to death. It was Saturday, January 27th.

For the king, life was as good as over. He had only to endure a little while, and his earthly task was ended. For Cromwell, the sternest work lay ahead.

In the anxious hours he spent with his son-in-law, Henry Ireton, he must have realized one thing above all. Whatever he did, he could not kill the King of England.

With Charles Stuart he could do as he willed. But the moment Charles was dead, another Charles, far away over the water and beyond Cromwell's power, would become King of England. This he must prevent if possible.

A law was hastily passed to make it high treason for anybody to proclaim any man King of England without the consent of Parliament. On the Monday other laws were passed. Nothing must be overlooked in the great changes Cromwell was bringing about.

Yet he was still having trouble with the judges. Some seemed strangely unwilling to sign the king's death warrant. Cromwell forced the pen into one man's hand and dragged him to the table.

There was some unseemly horseplay between them. Ink was spattered about, but Cromwell had the signature he wanted. Slowly the number of signatures grew until it took on some appearance of law.

Then the date and time of the execution were fixed. The king was to die on Tuesday, January 30, 1649, before the eyes of his people in Whitehall.

XI

The King Is Dead . . .

The night before his execution Charles asked if he might say farewell to his children. There were only two of them left in England. The Prince of Wales was safe in France, while his brother James had recently escaped from the palace, dressed in girl's clothes to outwit the sentries.

The Princess Elizabeth, aged thirteen, and her ten-year-old brother, the Duke of Gloucester, came full of grief to see their doomed father.

Charles greeted them tenderly, but he showed no weakness and expected none from them, young though they were. His greatest care was to see that his present sacrifice should not be in vain. Cromwell must not be allowed to make another king on his own account.

Charles spoke to the young Duke of Gloucester bluntly.

"They are going to cut off your father's head. Mark what I say! They will cut off my head and perhaps try to make you king. But you must never become king while your brothers, Charles and James, are alive. I charge you never to let them make you king."

The young boy looked his father bravely in the face.

"I will be torn in pieces first," he promised.

The king then blessed them both. He kissed them good-bye and gave to the princess two diamond seals in memory of him.

When she had departed sobbing, Charles said he would see nobody else. He needed the rest of his time for prayer.

Meanwhile, the Prince of Wales was making a last bid to save his father's life. He sent to Parliament a blank sheet of paper with his signature on it. They could fill in their own terms if only they would spare the king.

But nothing availed. Cromwell had been long in making up his mind. Now his determination was unshakable. The king must die if the peace of England was to be kept. He and his royal enemy were united in a single bond of duty. Each would do what he had to do for the generations to come.

On that last evening they nerved themselves for the final struggle. For the king, victory lay in dying bravely. For his enemies, the only hope was to weaken the king's courage.

If Charles but winced a little, if by his behavior on the scaffold he showed himself unworthy of the thousands who had died for him and because of him, the Crown would be tarnished for ever.

That may have been the reason why Charles was treated as he was next day. Perhaps muddled and nervousness were to blame. Either way it was unforgivable.

The king woke very early on that dark January morning of bitter cold. He dressed carefully, putting on two shirts lest he should shiver on the scaffold and so make people think that he was afraid to die.

He wore a black satin doublet and breeches, and over them a short velvet cloak. He also wore the blue ribbon of the Order of the Garter.

At eight o'clock he made his last communion. Bishop Juxon, a fine man who was liked by everybody, had brought him the bread and wine. He now remained with Charles to comfort his last moments.

In the House of Commons only a handful of members had assembled. It was freezing cold, and they must have been a miserable company. One member, who had stayed away, wrote later: "I went not to the house, but stayed all day at home and at my prayers, that this day's work might not so displease God as to bring prejudice to this poor afflicted nation."

Others were praying too, some silently as they stood

142

in Whitehall with their eyes on the soldiers taking up position. The troops were picked men who could be relied on to deal with the crowds if they tried to break loose.

It was Colonel Hacker who went along the frosty path to fetch Charles from the palace.

"Come, let us be going," said the king to Bishop Juxon.

The little procession set out along a route lined with foot soldiers, standing two deep. Behind the troops were the quiet crowds, shivering in the cruel weather.

But when Charles came to Whitehall he found that his executioners were not ready. He was kept waiting while the terrible day wore on. The regular headsman had refused to have anything to do with the business. A search for volunteers was in progress.

When at last two were found, they wore masks and disguised themselves with wigs and false beards. To this day we do not know for certain who they were.

In spite of everything the king kept his courage. Only one thing was troubling him. He was remembering the death of his great servant, the Earl of Strafford. Strafford had served Charles loyally, but the king had deserted him in his hour of need.

It was true that Strafford had told Charles to do so in order to save the crown. But Charles had never forgiven himself for his cowardice.

Now, in the early afternoon, he stepped forth to follow the path Strafford had trodden in the years gone by. He looked from the scaffold along Whitehall toward

143

the packed and silent Londoners. He saw that they were being kept too far away to hear anything he might say. Yet, in a calm voice, he began his speech.

He declared, as was true enough, that Parliament had really begun the war. He said, but it was false, that he had never meant to interfere with Parliament's privileges. He showed that his trial and sentence were unlawful, which was something that even Cromwell knew.

Toward the end he summed up what he believed, in these words:

"For the people, and truly I desire their liberty and freedom as much as anybody whomsoever, but I must tell you that their liberty and freedom consists in having, of government, those laws by which their life and their goods may be most their own.

"It is not for having a share in government, sirs; that is nothing pertaining to them. . . ."

So, to the last, Charles stood by his own ideas of government. It was for the king to decide what was good for his people. The people had no right to share in government.

Amid the multitude of causes for which Englishmen had shed each other's blood it was this one that really mattered. If the people were to have no say in lawmaking, they would be at the mercy of any tyrant who came to the throne. This was why the Civil War had been fought.

The king had only one more word to say. It was spoken not only to those around him but to those who were not yet born.

"Remember!"

The ax fell. A great groan of anguish went up from the people. Two troops of horse began to move along the street in opposite directions. The crowds scattered before their trampling hoofs. Oliver Cromwell was master of England.

There is a story told that during the following night a cloak and muffled figure was seen to approach the dead king; that it stood looking down on him for a long while and then slowly shook its head, sighing in a hollow voice the words, "Cruel necessity!"

The awestruck watchers swore that it was Cromwell himself, and it may well have been. The country squire whom troubled times had made into a great soldier was now being forced to play a fresh part.

He knew, better than most men, what he had done. He had set aside the laws of the realm. He had used armed force to drive out of Parliament all who disagreed with him. Now, with force alone, he had to rule the kingdom.

From that day on, he knew no peace. Time and again he tried to establish the rule of law, but none of the Parliaments he called could ever agree with him for long.

Some of the men who had helped in his rise to power also became his enemies. The Levelers mutinied in the army and had to be put down by force. On the walls of the church at Burford in Oxfordshire can be seen to this day the marks of the bullets Cromwell used against the rebels.

Inside, scratched on the font, one can read the pathetic words: *Antony Sedley — prisner, 1649.*

Men like the humble Sedley, however, were the least of Cromwell's foes. His great enemy was still King Charles and the memory of kingship he had left to his people and to his son.

That son was now himself a king. Charles the Second was growing into manhood in a foreign land. He was learning the bitter lessons of poverty and exile, but he was already meeting envoys from Scotland and planning his return.

He was hoping, as his father had hoped, to profit from the war in Ireland. Like his father he was disappointed by events in that distracted land. The Irish Catholics never had the chance to help him.

Cromwell crossed the Irish Sea in the summer of 1649 and began to wage war with a savage skill that the Irish remember to this day. Within a year, the peace of the sword had descended upon half the terrorized island. Then Cromwell departed, leaving Henry Ireton to finish off the rebels.

There was more fighting awaiting him in England for, on June 24, 1650, the new King Charles had landed in Scotland. News reached London that he was preparing to invade his southern kingdom. Parliament asked Fairfax to command the army against the Scots.

"Black Tom," however, had had enough. He resigned his command to Cromwell and retired into private life. Cromwell led the army north.

He did not mean to wait until the Scots were ready. On July 22nd he crossed the border with sixteen thousand men. Although the Scots had far more than that, they knew the quality of Cromwell's men.

They retreated slowly, laying waste their own country in an attempt to bring the English to a standstill. But sea power came to Cromwell's help and ships supplied the needs of his army.

At Dunbar he met the Scots in battle and defeated them utterly. Ten thousand prisoners were taken and hundreds of them sent off to the colonies of North America. Cromwell pursued his victorious way to Edinburgh and threatened to corner the new king.

It was now Christmas 1650, but a week later some of the Scots defiantly crowned Charles at Scone. It was an act that nobody could undo. The young man had become more dangerous than ever.

Before long he had a growing army and was looking southward to the border. On July 31, 1651, he dodged Cromwell and began his march on England. Cromwell followed a week later.

He was too late to prevent the young king from invading the southern kingdom. In all England there was no force of any size to oppose Charles. If the people rose in strength, the Roundhead cause might yet be lost.

With weaker forces shadowing him but powerless to halt him, Charles pressed on for the glittering prize that seemed his to take.

XII

... Long Live the King!

O n reaching England, Charles published a declaration to his people. He was ready to forgive and to forget, he said. He called on all his subjects to come to his defense.

The weakness of the response was almost unbelieveable. From a land which had raised thousands upon thousands to defend his father he received hardly a whisper of encouragement. Only a handful of volunteers came in. The English would not help the Scots.

148

The Earl of Derby scraped together fifteen hundred of his retainers but never had the chance to do more than that. Colonel Lilburne caught him at Wigan and smashed his force to pieces.

The young king had no choice but to go on. He marched along the borders of Wales, but the faithful Welshmen did not stir. Worse still, his army of Scots had begun to melt away.

By the time Charles reached Worcester he knew that he could go no farther. He began to fortify the city, hoping perhaps to hold out until the tardy English changed their minds.

They were given little time to do so. Cromwell reached Warwick with the main Roundhead army only two days later. There he found his subordinates, Lambert and Harrison, awaiting him. Between them, they had thirty thousand men.

It was enough not only to beat Charles but to destroy him. They laid their plans with care, so that there should be no escape.

Lambert was sent to block any retreat into Wales while Cromwell made ready his assault from the east. A bridge of boats was built across each of the rivers, Severn and Teme, which meet just below the city.

When all was ready, the first attack was launched along the west bank of the Severn. The Scots resisted so fiercely that Cromwell was forced to send reinforcements across his improvised bridge. The outnumbered Scots were then driven back into Worcester itself.

But this had weakened Cromwell's army on the east-

149

ern bank. Charles seized his opportunity to attack out of Worcester in that direction. Although he made headway, he was again checked by strong forces pouring back over the bridge of boats from the western bank. The Roundheads had laid their plans well.

Their greater skill and the experience of their men now began to tell. Charles was forced back into the city, with Cromwell storming after him. Again and again, the Scots rallied. Called to surrender and offered their lives, they replied with fresh volleys of musketry.

But their resistance could not last forever. The foot at length laid down their arms, while the horse made a supreme effort and managed to burst through the attackers. Charles fled with the rest.

The Roundhead victory was complete. By the next day Charles was a lonely fugitive with many miles of land and sea between himself and safety.

His army had ceased to exist. Only a handful of its pitiful survivors ever reached their homes. The Kingdom of Scotland could not find another army, and in April 1652 it submitted to English rule.

By that time Charles was safely back in France, but only after a long and adventurous journey. On the night after Worcester he had taken advantage of the darkness to shake off his companions.

"We had such a number of beaten horse with us," he said later, ". . . though I could not get them to stand by me against the enemy I could not get rid of them now I had a mind to it."

Perhaps Charles was joking when he said that. Those horsemen had fought bravely for him that day and were probably still trying to shield him by their presence. Neither he nor his father had ever had cause for complaint about their subjects' courage.

So it was now, as he began his wanderings through the countryside toward the distant sea. He was sheltered first by a family called Penderel, who were all risking their lives for him.

They dressed him in gray cloth breeches, a leather doublet and a green jerkin. His hair was ravaged by clumsy scissors and his face and hands blackened with soot. Accompanied by Richard Penderel, he hid the first day in a little wood while Cromwell's soldiers were searching for him everywhere.

They had posted a notice for him, offering a reward for his capture and describing him as being a tall man, "above two yards high."

That night he tried to make for Wales, where he hoped to find a ship for France. He traveled seven miles and then hid in a barn all next day. Finding that the River Severn was too closely guarded to be crossed in safety he returned to the Penderels at Boscobel House.

But it was not safe to stay there either, so on the following day he took his famous refuge in the oak tree. He was perched there, hidden in its thick summer greenness, when the men who were searching for him passed beneath its branches.

At night he returned to rest at Boscobel House, while the Penderel family stayed on guard, ready to rouse him if anybody came near.

After several days he decided it was safe to make another move. With four of the Penderels escorting

151

him, he went on to Moseley, about six miles away, where he found Lord Wilmot also in hiding.

There he had a piece of luck. A young lady called Jane Lane happened to be in the neighborhood. She had with her a pass to take her into the west of England, with a servingman in attendance. It was soon arranged that the King of England should become the servingman.

He took the name of William Jackson and set out with his young mistress. They went by way of Stratford-on-Avon and Cirencester until they came to Bristol. Although Charles was recognized at least once on this journey, he was not betrayed even for the thousand pounds that Parliament was now offering for his capture.

From Bristol, where he failed to find a ship, Charles wandered with Mistress Lane through Somerset and into Dorset. Here they parted company, for Charles had found other friends to help him.

He had arranged to wait for Lord Wilmot at Bridport and it was this which nearly cost him his freedom. When he reached Bridport he found it full of troops and was tempted to withdraw. But to do so would have meant leaving Wilmot in the lurch.

He went boldly to the best inn in the town and found its courtyard crowded with soldiers. Charles dismounted and led his horse right between the soldiers toward the stable. He pushed them aside so rudely that they turned and shouted at him for his clumsiness.

But there was no hope of a ship in Dorset, so he began with Wilmot to make his way along the south coast in the direction of Dover. At one place his cropped hair excited the anger of some fierce Royalist who nearly beat him for being a Roundhead.

Escaping all dangers, he at last reached Brighton. There he spent the night at the George Inn, where he was again recognized but not betrayed. Even after that there was more danger, this time from the master of the ship which had been hired to take him abroad.

The sailor recognized him, and was frightened. He knew he had been hired to help a Royalist but he had not known it was Charles. To aid the king's escape meant to risk his neck and he began to complain that Wilmot had not played fair with him.

Charles exerted all his charm. He sat with the man all night, drinking and smoking with him so that he should not have a chance to change his mind. The next morning the ship sailed and arrived in Normandy on October 16th. The king was safe at last.

Not for eight more years of poverty and anxiety did he return to England. In those years the country became a Commonwealth and Oliver Cromwell became the Lord Protector of it. But try as he would Cromwell could not stamp out the memory of kingship.

The king at last came into his own again and tried in turn to stamp out the memory of Cromwell. But that could not be done either.

Charles the First and his great enemy had done their

153

work well. Between them, they had sketched out the shape of England's future, although in their day neither of them could see it.

It is not given to any of us to know what would have happened if they had acted in some other way. But it is surely no accident that Britons are still subjects of a kingdom.

In other lands where there was no Cromwell to outface the Crown, where there was no brave and lonely king to leave his memory, the people turned away from monarchy forever.

England owes to Charles, to Cromwell, to all those simple men who fought and died, and to all the women and children who bore the hardships of siege and bombardment, a debt that can never be repaid.

There is in the gray old city of London, an annual event which reminds England of Charles and Cromwell. On the present queen's birthday, the royal guards march across their parade ground in the ceremony of Trooping the Color.

When they do it they are paying honor to the descendant of King Charles, but they are wearing the red coats of the New Model Army.

Index

155

The Author

SUTHERLAND ROSS developed his interest in history as a boy when the local blacksmith told him about the *Mayflower*. It has been unabated since then. The author, an English citizen, is a schoolmaster in London and has written twelve juvenile books.